# Talk that Matters

# Talk that Matters

## 30 Days *to* Better Relationships

**Susan Lee Lind, PhD**
**and**
**Ben Campbell Johnson, PhD**

FRESH AIR BOOKS®
Nashville

Cover design: Left Coast Design, Portland, Oregon
Interior design and layout: Perfectype
Cover illustration: Krieg Barrie, Hoquiam, Washington
First printing: 2009

LIBRARY OF CONGRESS CATALOGING-IN-PUBLICATION DATA

Lind, Susan Lee, 1950–

    Talk that matters / by Susan Lee Lind and Ben Campbell Johnson.

      p. cm.

    ISBN: 978-1-935205-03-6

1. Communication in marriage. 2. Couples—Psychology. 3. Man-woman relationships. I. Johnson, Ben Campbell. II. Title.

    HQ734.L5659  2009

    646.7'8—dc22                            2008042760

Printed in the United States of America

To our parents

*Fred and Cammie Johnson*

and

*Harry and Marjorie Kone*

# Contents

# Preface

This book is for people who are weary of superficial talk and want to build meaningful relationships through thoughtful conversation. It is not about chatter, gossip, or small talk. You can get that kind of talk without much effort. Meaningless talk comes easily, requiring little thought and virtually no preparation.

We believe that people prefer a way of talking that builds enduring relationships, but they simply do not know how to talk in order to achieve this goal. In these pages, we present an approach that will help our readers learn the art of clear, effective communication. Will it take some work? Yes! Will it mean changes in the perception of yourself and others? You bet! Will it mean learning some new ways to listen and to speak? Count on it! The good news is this: if you will learn these new ways of listening to people and new ways of talking with them, you will begin to experience significant improvements in your relationships.

Since personal relationships occur in a number of settings, we have chosen different contexts in which to illustrate the basic principles for *Talk That Matters*. These principles apply to husbands, wives, lovers, friends, employees, employers, parents, children, and casual acquaintances.

We offer you a way to get started with basic principles that make meaningful talk possible, insights that make it smoother, and ways to recognize differences in people that will help with the larger issues needing clear speech like openness, honesty, forgiveness, and love. To present this material, we have written short lessons for easy reading and step-by-step progress. Each part states a principle, illustrates it, and suggests a way to practice it. Everything in this book is simple, practical, easy-to-understand, and possible to do. Want to be a more perceptive person who adds to the fullness of life for yourself and others? You can be!

While writing this book, we had the idea that people seeking meaningful talk would read a principle each day and practice that principle by observing or engaging in conversation in new ways. The book is small, the principles simple (but not necessarily easy); each day provides an opportunity to work with a particular task.

We write from firsthand experience. These principles changed our lives as we practiced them. Our relationships with our spouses have been enriched, and our relationships with others have become more open and free. In addition, we believe that this kind of talk has made us healthier, more competent people. We both know the other side of talk that matters—shallow talk, conflicted talk, unheard talk, meaningless talk. So we deeply desire to offer a means to liberate people who are stuck in painful, frustrating, confusing, and destructive relationships because they do not know how to talk when the talk matters.

We believe that this book can give you needed skills for a richer, more meaningful life.

Susan Lee Lind, PhD<br>
Ben Campbell Johnson, PhD

# Before You Begin

ommunication has been around since our cave brothers and sisters drew on walls and grunted and gestured at one another. We like to think we have come a long way from those days; some of us even like to think we have turned communication into an art form. But have we come as far as all that? How much have we really learned about communicating with each other? A look at the state of our relationships will provide a clue. "How many American marriages end in divorce? One in two, if you believe the statistic endlessly repeated in news media reports, academic papers, and campaign speeches."[1] A 50 percent divorce rate is one telltale sign of misunderstood wishes, missed opportunities, and conflicted communication. Broken friendships and unhappy employees additionally illustrate that we may not have made as much progress as we imagine.

So, although this book is not a treatise on communication or the psychology of communication, it is a guide designed to give you the fundamental tools you need to communicate more effectively with the people around you—your family, friends, bosses, and colleagues. And you can do it in thirty days if you

- really want to improve your relationships,
- follow our principle-a-day format, and
- practice the exercises at the end of each principle on a daily basis.

Think about it—thirty days to better communication! So if that is what you want, we offer a simple yet powerful model of communication on which we hang our tips, techniques, and exercises.

Our model of communication contains four basic elements: a sender, a message, a receiver, and feedback to the sender.

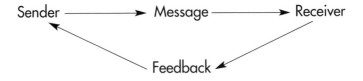

This simple model can work for you. Potentially, it offers you a life of greater insight, less pain, and deeper fulfillment in all your relationships. In the pages that follow, we will explore each element of this model by offering definitions, explanations, and illustrations.

Our book is arranged for you to learn a principle a day. In thirty days you can have the tools you need to engage in talk that matters. Each principle is simple and easy to comprehend. Read a different one each day; understand it, practice it, and make that principle your own. We have structured these principles from the basic to the more complex so that they build on one another. If you need or want more time to practice a particular principle, feel free to take that time, then jump back in and tackle the next one.

Do you want to grow in your ability to communicate? Then take that all-important step—begin the *Talk That Matters* journey and stick to it for thirty days!

# DAY 1

## Discover where you are.

The first step in any personal improvement process is to be aware of where you are now. How well do you communicate with others? Are you clear and concise? Do you listen? Are you aware of how your communication impacts others?

If you repeatedly hear comments and questions like the following, they may indicate your current communication state.

*From a fellow worker:* "Where are you today? Your head seems to be in the clouds."

*From a friend:* "I don't feel like we're on the same page. Is something wrong? Is there a problem?"

*From a spouse or significant other:* "You're always talking and never listening to me. I don't feel very important when you don't listen to me."

*From your boss:* "You don't seem to be listening when I tell you what to do. What is going on in that head of yours?"

If you hear questions and comments like these, you may be passing through life in a communication haze, unaware of the impact your communication practices have on others and on you.

If you could choose between going through life in a haze or being awake and aware, which would you choose? If you were passing through life oblivious to your friends, insensitive to the needs of others, unaware of the beauty around you, would you want someone to point out what you were missing?

> **If you could choose between going through life in a haze or being awake and aware, which would you choose?**

Marie and Tom, friends who haven't seen each other in three months, have a lot of catching up to do. Tom gives Marie an open ear for thirty minutes—maybe more. Finally, Tom gets a chance to speak. He says only a few words before Marie takes over the conversation again. This pattern persists the whole evening, and Tom's time to talk never comes. When the two friends part, Tom leaves feeling unfulfilled and hurt.

Think about the person in your life who seems to be unconcerned about your ideas, wishes, or needs. When you are with this person, does he or she

- always talk about himself or herself?
- never ask about you?
- seem uninterested in what you say?
- begin talking before you complete a sentence?
- play one-upmanship?
- discount your contribution to the relationship with silence or rejection?

Focus for a moment on how this behavior makes you feel. Unless you know how to evaluate it, you probably get negative messages that evoke unpleasant feelings. You may feel

- ignored
- discounted
- unappreciated
- estranged
- bored
- angry

You meet men and women like this in social gatherings, in families, at dinners with friends. You run into them at conferences, on the subway and in airplanes, and even at religious gatherings. Being reared in a good home, having a responsible position in a company, attending the "right" cocktail parties, or dating the most beautiful or handsome person does not guarantee communication savvy.

So what is really going on with folks who dominate conversations? You might think they are egocentric and selfish. Maybe they are just afraid to listen to others because of what they might hear. Or maybe they need to maintain control of the situation by doing all the talking. Most of these "I'm center-stage" people have no idea how they are interacting with people, how they are perceived, or what they are missing.

Consider how much people miss in life when they live unaware of the needs and feelings of others. We who have escaped from this prison can tell you that being locked up inside yourself is lonely. You are afraid most of the time—afraid to look inside and afraid that you are so transparent that others already see through you. This anxiety constantly fuels internal feelings about what others might say. Not seeing and not feeling leads to numbness and unbearable loneliness. Furthermore, your frustration in these relationships blocks your ability to talk in a way that matters.

Is it possible to escape this predicament? Yes, but it takes work. Here are three simple guidelines to help you change unawareness to aliveness and connection.

1. *Stop.* Most of us are running so fast that we end up with automated living and programmed conversations. We do not have time to think or weigh alternatives; our wheels are turning too fast. We have no time to think about what is precious to us, how we want to value and respond to others, or what goals we want to pursue.

Pause for a minute. Put your mind in park. Be still. If stillness is a new experience for you, it may help to tell your body to be quiet, relax, and settle down. Close your eyes and allow the tension to drain from your body. Take three to five deep breaths and hold on to the quiet for a few seconds longer. *If you want to discover where you are in these important relationships, stop!*

2. *Look.* Look at your life. Examine your schedule for the past few days. Ask yourself, *What is going on in my significant relationships?* Look at both your communication and that of the people close to you. Do you listen? Do you continually change the focus of conversation to yourself? Do you interrupt? Do they? Five minutes of observing will yield a wealth of information. *If you wish to escape blocked relations, look!*

3. *Listen.* Listen to the sounds around you—birds chirping, people talking, planes flying overhead, cell phones ringing. Go within yourself and listen to the static in your mind—to the fears and questions that pop up—to your yearnings. This simple exercise will bring you to the present. Really listen to the people who are in your life daily. Hear what they are saying or trying to say to you. *If you desire to live in the present moment, listen!*

●　　●　　●

Stop! Look! Listen! Set aside fifteen minutes today to practice these three steps. If you want to change your communication style, you can.

Remember, talk that matters begins with knowing where you are in the art of communication.

## My Wake-Up Scale

On a scale from 1 to 10, with 10 being the highest, how strongly do you feel about removing the haze and awakening to life? Circle a number.

1    2    3    4    5    6    7    8    9    10

# DAY 2

## Send a clear message.

**A**lmost everyone wants to be understood, but sometimes the easy flow of information gets blocked when communication is vague, ambiguous, or disguised. For example:

*To a friend:* "Why don't you have time to go to the movies anymore?"

*To a business associate:* "Why aren't you taking care of our better customers like Meyer? Our business has dropped 20 percent."

*To a spouse:* "Why don't we make love anymore—like we used to?"

These conversation openers invite a fight. These questions carry a tone of blame and will likely evoke negative responses. Once the ambiguous question gets a negative response, bad feelings arise; false assumptions are made; and the communicators become estranged.

In the three negative attempts at communication above, the sender does not identify his or her thoughts, does not own his or her feelings, and does not express his or her desire clearly. How might these conversations have gotten off to a better start? The speaker needs to send clear messages about his or her wants, feelings, or needs. The following suggestions will help you communicate clearly with others:

> State your message clearly.... Own your desires.

- State your message using concrete, unambiguous words.
- Own your desires by making "I" statements; avoid using "we," "they," "some people say," or "others think." For example:

*To a friend you say:*
"I'd like to go to a movie tonight. Can you come with me?"
*Response:* "That's a great idea. I've been studying like crazy, and that would be fun. What do you want to see?"

*To a business associate you say:*
"I know that we've been neglecting the Meyer account. What do you say we call on the president today?"
*Response:* "I agree, but today won't work for me. What about next Monday? Is that soon enough?"

*To your spouse you say:*
"We've both been so busy I'd like a little together time tonight. What about you?"
*Response:* "I'd like that too."

All of these statements are clear. They place desires and feelings on the table and allow for the making of constructive decisions.

Why don't we send clear messages? It might be because of the following:

- our cultural origins or societal norms
- long-standing habits of personal interaction
- fear of rejection or exposure
- confusion about our thoughts, feelings, and beliefs

Doug was reared in a family that made suggestions and gave directives by asking questions. But the questions disguised the real motives. When Doug's mom said, "Wouldn't you like to go to the beach today?" she expected the answer to be yes. Doug grew up in this communication environment knowing that the question was not really a question—it was a directive.

After Doug married and had a family, Doug's mom asked her daughter-in-law, "Sharon, wouldn't it be nice for us to celebrate Christmas together this year?" Sharon did not understand the code, so she replied, "Actually, I'd rather stay home with the children this Christmas." The atmosphere grew a little tense after her response, and Sharon did not know why. She mistakenly thought the question was a real question when in fact it was a directive.

Early on, Doug learned from his mom to ask questions instead of making clear, self-revealing statements to express his needs and wants. He often repeated this pattern of communication with Sharon. To avoid tension in their relationship, Sharon needed to adopt the same code or ask Doug to state his thoughts and feelings clearly and drop the questions. This habit of hiding his feelings also flowed over into Doug's friendships and work relations. The habit, while innocent enough, created ambiguity and confusion.

Maybe Doug's communication style came from his desire not to offend others. Others might interpret a clear, concise, and direct statement as cold, brazen, or controlling. To mask a desire with a question softens the impact, but it also confuses the communication.

Hiding a desire behind a question, however, makes rejection less likely. We think, *If I don't tell them what I honestly want, they can't reject me!*

At some time in her early life, Doug's mom probably stated a feeling or a desire and had it trounced on. She learned that being open and honest brought her pain, so she began to shield herself with questions.

People also send vague, ambiguous, and disguised messages because they lack clarity about their desires. A clouded, confused person cannot send a clear, unambiguous message. To send a clear message, do the following:

- Name your expected outcome.
- State your message clearly.
- Claim the desire as your own.

To name your expected outcome, slow down enough to sort out your feelings or wishes. Identify the one issue you wish to express. To state your message clearly, use few words and keep it short and to the point.

To own your message, use "I" language. For example, use "I think," "I feel," or "I want." Avoid the plurals, "we" or "they" or "some people."

This way of stating what you want may at first seem abrasive or even frightening, but being understood requires straightforward speech. You may soften your talk by the tone of your voice, your posture, and your facial expressions. Showing a willingness to listen and negotiate will also ensure that the hearer receives your message.

●　　●　　●

Today observe the communication patterns of those with whom you interact. Pay particular attention when you hear people say "we" or "some people" when they mean "I." Why do they mask their desires or ideas?

- Is it cultural origin or societal norms?
- Is it habit?
- Is it a fear of rejection?
- Is it confusion about what they believe?

Become aware of your own style of sending messages. In a safe environment, practice identifying your desire or intention. State it clearly and succinctly, taking ownership of it.

For example, you might say to your loved one, "I would appreciate some time with you tonight." To a child you can say, "I want you to come straight home from school, do your homework, and help me prepare dinner." In each of these examples, you state your desire and leave the door open for discussion.

*Score yourself.* On a scale of 1 to 10, rate your clarity of communication today with 1 being poor and 10 perfection.

1    2    3    4    5    6    7    8    9    10

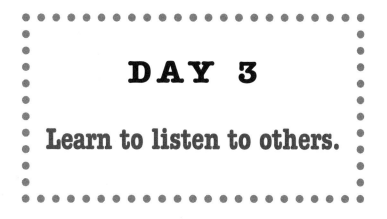

# DAY 3

## Learn to listen to others.

If you do not listen, another's words cannot span the space between you. It takes time to learn to listen, but it is worth the effort. This principle is for you if you could be more attentive to the people around you, or you want to pay attention to others but do not know how.

Have you ever heard the term *people-listening*? It is similar to *people-watching*, with the added benefit of discovering what is going on in your world and in the worlds of the people who talk to you.

People-listening takes effort. You may feel that you do not have the time to listen and may also believe it is not really necessary. After all, if you are the boss at work, others *should* automatically listen to you. Or, if you are a parent, your spouse and children *should* listen to you. You can probably think of other situations where you believe your role commands people to listen to you. Well, it is time to shatter this illusion!

Listening is not automatic. You cannot demand it and ensure that people will listen to you. People listen to you because they *want* to listen to you. And you listen to others because you *want* to listen to them. Good listening is a gift, freely and willingly offered without payment. You can give it, and you can receive it.

So, what is people-listening? First of all, it differs from hearing. Hearing is the biological function of picking up sound vibrations. You hear a bird's chirp, a computer's whir, or a cell phone's ring. Unless the sounds annoy you, you identify them, attach meaning to them, and then dismiss them. They go in one ear and out the other.

> Listening is not automatic. . . . Good listening is a gift. . . . You can give it, and you can receive it.

People-listening, on the other hand, requires something of you: time, energy, and a willingness to stay focused on the other person. So how can you do this?

First, you have to *want* to listen. If you do not care about what another is saying and what she means by her words, you will not listen. So think about how you might benefit from listening—whether it is to understand, to show respect, to get clear instructions, or to build a relationship.

Second, you must commit to listen. A commitment is a deliberate choice to focus on the other person's words, tone, and body language. The more committed you are to the task, the more you will enjoy the results. The commitment requires effort and hard work. You have the ability to listen, but do you also have the commitment? If you are unsure and want to check your commitment level, select a level on the following list, "My Commitment to Listen to Others."

## My Commitment to Listen to Others

| | |
|---|---|
| Penthouse | I did |
| Level 9 | I will |
| Level 8 | I can |
| Level 7 | I think I can |
| Level 6 | I might |
| Level 5 | I think I might |
| Level 4 | What is it? |
| Level 3 | I wish I could |
| Level 2 | I don't know how |
| Level 1 | I can't |
| Ground Floor | I won't |

Mark your current commitment to listening. Unless you are already there, commit to working your way up to the penthouse!

•   •   •

Today notice what your mind does when someone is talking to you. Record your observations here:

# DAY 4

## Learn the rules of good listening.

There are rules for good listening just as there are rules for good writing, good negotiating, and good driving. To listen perceptively, learn the rules. The level of your own commitment to listen to others that you selected in the previous lesson tells you something about your intent, but it does not tell you how to go about people-listening. Here are some ideas:

1. *Make eye contact.* A good way to start improving your communication skills is to look directly at the other person. What color eyes does he or she have? Are they blue or green or brown or gray or something altogether different? When you can answer this question, you know you have made eye contact.

What is so important about making eye contact? In Western society, it makes people feel valued and respected. We look someone in the eyes to determine if he or she is trustworthy or indifferent. Remember the adage "The eyes are the mirror of the soul"? Or the term *shifty-eyed*?

Remember as a child being told by an authority figure to "look me in the eyes, and tell me the truth"? The implication of that saying was that if you could not look the person in the eyes, you must be hiding something.

Lack of eye contact, however, can also signal shyness, embarrassment, indifference, boredom—and in some cultures, respect. Eye contact doesn't communicate the same intent in all cultures. But our discussion here on eye contact and nonverbal behavior relates specifically to Western society. How do you feel when a store clerk ignores you without giving you even a glance? You may feel dismissed or devalued because eye contact is critical to the listening process. How much eye contact do you give people: none, some, too little, or too much? If your eye contact is too intense, it can feel intrusive. Instead, look between the person's eyes or at his or her nose or chin so that it doesn't become awkward. Never gaze at someone more than twenty seconds; any longer becomes an unwelcome stare.

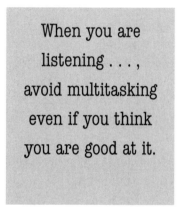

**When you are listening . . . , avoid multitasking even if you think you are good at it.**

2. *Pay attention.* When you are listening to someone, avoid multitasking even if you think you are good at it. It can communicate boredom or disinterest. Put yourself in this scene. At work, you have been putting out one fire after another. You finally have a few minutes to get organized for the next day when one of your employees pops into your office to ask some questions about a project. You continue checking your e-mail and thumbing through your inbox while he tries to talk to you. What do you think might happen as a result of your behavior?

- The employee feels you are not giving him the time and attention he deserves.
- You agree to an action you later regret (like adding staff).

- You overlook faulty or misleading information that could come back to haunt you.

If you said all three, you are right. All are possible outcomes of multitasking instead of people-listening.

The same counsel about multitasking applies if you are at home. Let's say your daughter wants to talk to you. Do you continue watching TV and thumbing through the mail while your child tries to chat? If you do, what message are you sending? Your actions say that your activities are more important than she is. Your daughter sees that other matters take priority. Do you think she will want to chat again? If you miss this chance to give your daughter your undivided attention, the opportunity might not come again.

3. *Watch your nonverbal behavior.* As you listen, do you glance at your watch or the clock on the wall or roll your eyes or tap your fingers on your desk? All these nonverbal behaviors (also called visual behaviors or body language) signal boredom. When have you exhibited these behaviors? What happened? Boredom might not be your intent, but it will be your message. Your body language speaks so loudly that the sender does not hear what you say but only sees what you do.

Keep in mind the **3 Vs of Communication**:

- **V**isual (nonverbal behavior)
- **V**erbal (words and language)
- **V**ocal (tone, tempo, rhythm, and volume)

Each of these components has an impact on your *believability*. The diagram on the next page indicates that actual words contribute only 7 percent to the effectiveness of your communication. Your vocal tone contributes 38 percent, and your nonverbal behavior contributes a whopping 55 percent. When all three Vs are in sync and reinforce one another, your message is believed. However, if your tone and body language differ from your words, your listener will believe your tone and body language over your words. Think about it. Ninety-three percent of what people believe is based on how you **look** and how you **sound**, not on what you **say**.

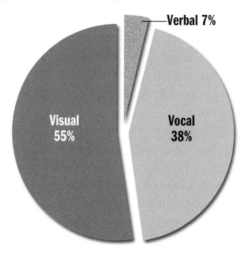

*Based on a study by Albert Mehrabian published in* Silent Messages[1]

Here is a scenario. You are angry with an associate for making a decision that creates more work for the people you supervise and for not involving you in the decision. Your people are already pressed with work covering for Mary, who is out on maternity leave. Rather than confronting your colleague, expressing your anger, and trying to solve the problem, you take another route. When you encounter him in the elevator, you say sarcastically, "My people have all the time in the world to do this additional work, especially with Mary out on maternity leave and, incidentally, thanks a lot for including me in the decision-making process." The elevator door opens at your floor; you give your colleague a withering look and abruptly walk out.

Which of the 3 Vs do you think your colleague is going to believe—your words, the Verbal; the tone of your voice, the Vocal; or your non-verbal behavior, the Visual? You are right if you said Vocal and Visual.

Even though your words told your colleague all is well, the sarcasm and the body language gave a very different message.

4. *Focus on what the other person is saying.* As you listen, focus on the other person's ideas, feelings, and beliefs rather than your own. It is easy to slip into focusing on yourself and your beliefs or to concentrate on what you are going to say next.

Here is another scenario. Your spouse is trying to tell you about her day. You interrupt her to say, "You think you've had it tough; you're not going to believe what happened to me today." Guess what? Your people-listening skills just went out the window. Rather than receiving the communication, you have shifted the focus to yourself. You have intercepted her conversation and have begun running toward your own goal. Your behavior tells your spouse that you are really more important than she is.

Instead of rushing to speak, take a deep breath, close your mouth, and listen to what your spouse thinks, feels, and believes about her day. Hear her out. Really listen to what she is saying. Reflect a feeling she is expressing. For example, "It sounds like that really frustrated you." Paraphrase her message if you feel unclear. You might ask, "Are you saying you're frustrated?" Or, you could ask for clarification: "Are you frustrated?"

Paraphrasing your wife's words lets her know that you are paying attention and really want to understand her point of view. You might also say, "So, if I understand you correctly, you want . . ." or "So you mean that . . ." or "To put that another way, you feel . . ." Don't speak until she stops talking. Don't interrupt, finish her sentence, or talk over her words. Your ideas will not vanish. Your feelings will not evaporate. Your beliefs will not take a holiday. Keep them in check until your spouse finishes, and then proceed.

As you listen, try to acknowledge that the message your spouse is sending is about her. The message is not about you; it is about her. So avoid taking the message personally. This understanding is fundamental to authentic communication. How many times have you been upset because you have misinterpreted an offhanded comment and taken it personally? For example, on a visit to your home, your brother-in-law says to you, "We keep the dogs outside because of Martha's allergies to the hair and dander." He is not telling you what to do with your dog. Take it at face value. Do not jump to a conclusion and assume he is slamming you for allowing your dog inside. He is concerned about your sister and her comfort. Remember that the message is about your brother-in-law and your sister and not about you. So avoid getting your nose out of joint by assuming his intent.

To recap, the four rules of good listening are these:

1. Make eye contact.
2. Pay attention.
3. Watch your nonverbal behavior.
4. Focus on what the other person is saying.

● ● ●

Today pick two people in your world (one at work and one at home), and diligently apply the four rules above. Listen to their ideas, thoughts, beliefs, feelings, passions, questions, concerns, and problems. As a people-listener, raise questions to clarify, reflect feelings, and paraphrase thoughts. Also, listen to what they are *not* saying. Be attentive to their body language. Pick up on cues they may be giving that will help you listen better. In the space below describe what happened.

# DAY 5

## Write a clear message.

Written communication such as e-mails, letters, proposals, and reports are frequently fragmented; miscommunication occurs. There are 4 Cs you can apply to ensure that your written message communicates. The essence of your communication resides in the designed and detailed content of your message, so apply the 4 Cs when creating your message.

To master the **4 Cs of Communication**, be

- Clear
- Correct
- Concise
- Complete

Usually simple messages are the best. They are direct, well thought through, and can be received as they are intended. But many messages are clouded with innuendo, flowery phrases, and/or words with negative or confusing connotations. For your message to reach your receiver with clarity, you will need to consider the 4Cs every time you prepare to deliver your message.

1.  Is what you are communicating clear, easy to understand, and digestible in small bites?
2.  Is your message correct? Does it explain with detailed accuracy? Are you using the language correctly?
3.  Is your message concise and to the point? Is it sharply focused and stating what you want to say in an uncluttered style?
4.  Are you saying or communicating everything that is essential to the message? Is it complete? Will your receivers understand the content because you have not left anything out?

Your colleague Ms. Morris leaves you an e-mail message:

I'm coming to Paris in June, and I'll see you then. My assistant has the travel details. I'll have her call you. I'm looking forward to this trip and hope to see you sometime after I arrive at de Gaulle. Maybe I'll call you when I get in, and we can connect. See you soon.

The message seems disjointed and unclear. Here is the same message, carefully considered.

I am leaving New York Kennedy Airport on June 14 and will arrive in Paris on June 15 at 8:00 in the morning, Paris time.

My plane will arrive at Charles de Gaulle Airport, and I will need someone to pick me up at the Delta arrival center.

My flight is Delta #17, scheduled to arrive at de Gaulle at 7:44 a.m., Paris time.

I will be traveling alone. I will have one checked bag and one piece of carry-on luggage.

I will be staying at the George V. Hotel at 31, avenue George V. The telephone number at the hotel is 47.23.54.00. I have made arrangements for early check-in.

I'm looking forward to seeing you on the 15th of June.

The second message is longer than the first, but its precise information leaves the receiver with little doubt about the intent. It is clear, correct, concise, and complete. Concise does not always mean short. The first communication, although containing fewer sentences, is shy on information and detail—detail that could easily have been included with some thought. It also leaves the receiver with a number of questions requiring follow-up.

How important is the message? Very.

Consider the times you have received information that you believed to be true and accurate, only to learn that it wasn't. It might have been related to an appointment or information about directions to a restaurant. In each instance, the message lacked clarity and caused you some aggravation. How can you avoid experiencing this kind of communication? What can you do to make your written messages clear, correct, concise, and complete? Here are some guidelines for your e-mails, letters, proposals, reports, and other written communication.

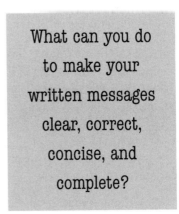

What can you do to make your written messages clear, correct, concise, and complete?

# Guidelines for written communication

1. Write out your message.
2. Edit what you have written.
3. Have someone else read it for clarity and accuracy.
4. Revise.
5. Read it aloud, then put it aside.
6. Read it again later in the day.
7. If you have time, let it sit overnight and then read it the next day.
8. Look at your message one last time and then. . . .
9. Send your message.

This nine-step process seems like a lot, but if you want your messages to be well communicated and well received, it takes some work. As you use this procedure, it will become easier. The more you do it, the more you will be able to do it well—and quickly. It gives structure to your message and provides you with a format for ensuring that your message is correctly structured, that you have met the 4Cs, and that you will reach your receiver the way you intended.

●   ●   ●

Today try this exercise: Write a clear message to a colleague, friend, or family member. Apply the nine-step process as outlined above. Ask for feedback on how clear, concise, correct, and complete your message is.

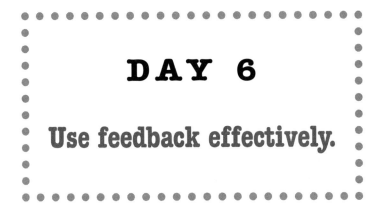

# DAY 6

## Use feedback effectively.

**F**eedback is the receiver's response to the sender's message. It is also the last component in our communication model (see page 12). So far, you have practiced speaking and sending a message. You have learned a nine-step process for composing your message. And you have experienced the benefits of listening as the receiver of a message. These basic practices will guarantee clarity and will change your way of thinking, speaking, and listening.

The sixth principle requires using feedback effectively. Feedback, the receiver's response to the sender's message, is a vital component in our communication model for two reasons. First, it quickly broadcasts to the sender whether the receiver is getting the sender's intended message. Second, it quickly pivots the sender into the role of receiver.

This dynamic is important both to sender and receiver in order to keep the communication on track. The original sender must listen for and pay attention to the feedback, interpret the feedback, and then, if necessary, change his or her message or delivery to accommodate the feedback. If ignored, the communication could derail; without feedback, no correction is possible. The dynamic of sender becoming receiver and receiver becoming sender is what makes this particular model of communication so simple yet effective.

What form does this feedback take? Feedback can be any combination of verbal, vocal, and visual cues—the three Vs of communication we talked about in Day 4. Smiling and nodding with full attention alerts the sender that the receiver is on the same track. If the sender senses, sees, or hears anything else—for example, a quizzical look, a frown, a question—then adjustments to the message or the delivery need to be made. The sender's goal is to have the message interpreted as intended. And feedback is critical to the process.

> **Feedback can be any combination of verbal, vocal, and visual cues.**

Let's say you intend to give explicit directions to your neighbor, Pete, about driving to a local restaurant. As you speak, you notice a quizzical look on his face and then see him frown. What might be your best response? Previously, you may not have even noticed Pete's nonverbal cues and instead rushed on with your explanation. But let's say you do notice Pete's confusion. Would you continue? Or, would you pause and ask Pete if the directions made sense?

To use feedback effectively, take in the responses as helpful information, and respond accordingly. Don't just continue talking. Change your behavior; do something different. Feedback from Pete is telling you that he does not understand your directions. So stop and try this:

1. *Make an observation*: "From the look on your face, Pete, I can see I'm confusing you."
2. *Ask a question*: "Would writing down the directions help?"

The mother-daughter telephone conversation below illustrates back-and-forth feedback:

**Mother**: Betsy, you really should stop smoking. I've just read another article about the hazards of cigarette smoking. It talked about the negative effects that smoking has on women with Crohn's disease. With your condition, you're putting yourself at risk. You're going to kill yourself before you're fifty and leave your husband and son to fend for themselves. How can you do that to people you love?

**Daughter**: Mother, will you quit nagging and leave me alone? How many more times are you going to be on my case? I know it's bad, but I've told you before that it relaxes me and controls my weight. The last time I stopped smoking, I gained twenty pounds. I'm not going to gain weight like that again; it was too hard to lose. So will you just back off?

**Mother**: Well, if that's the way you're going to be, all right. I'll just throw the article away or send it to someone who cares about her health.

**Daughter**: Oh, Mother, you just don't understand!

**Mother**: Of course I understand. I understand all too well that smoking will kill you, and you refuse to do anything about it.

**Daughter**: I've had enough, Mother. I'm hanging up now.

Betsy and her mother have had this conversation more than once. And neither one has changed her mind. Both are responding to each other in the same way they have responded in the past, resulting in the same kind of conversation and dual frustration.

Think about this type of failure in another setting—golf. If your putting stroke is causing the ball to go left of the hole, but you continue to use the same stroke, what is going to happen? The ball will continue to go left because you did not make any adjustment in your stroke. The same concept applies to Betsy and her mother. Neither one is using feedback to adjust her communication style. So they get the same result.

In your interactions with others do you expect different results without making any adjustments in the way you communicate? When you are the communicator and want to get your message across, it is your responsibility to communicate in a way that your listener can understand. If the feedback from your listener is not what you want or expect, you—not your listener—are responsible for changing the way your message is delivered. The sender is responsible for making the message understandable to the listener.

For some people, taking responsibility for communication is a new idea and one that is not always willingly embraced. It forces you to account for what comes out of your mouth. It forces you to engage your brain and choose your words consciously. It is easy to react out of ego or emotion and say unguarded and destructive words. Dealing with feedback takes thought, time, and attention.

You have probably heard the adage "Think before you speak." When you do not consciously consider what you are saying, you likely will react out of your own values, beliefs, and feelings without considering your partner's particular views, values, and needs. To frame your communication so that another can hear it, pay attention to the feedback you receive.

●   ●   ●

Take a quick self-test to help you evaluate how conscious you are of using feedback effectively. Think of a person either at work or at home whose feedback you have difficulty understanding. Ask yourself the following questions with this person in mind:

1.  What are the circumstances of the situation? What are the issues that brought me to this point? Why am I in the situation that I am in with this person?

2.  What kind of relationship do I have with this person? Intimate? Rocky? Distant? Anxious? Loving? Strained? New? Quickly

turned sour? Long term? Sibling? Spouse? Parent-Child? Significant other? In-law? Stepchild?

3. What outcome do I want from the interaction? from the relationship?

4. What types of personalities are involved? Introverts? Extroverts? Are we more similar or different?

5. Have I anticipated how this person might think, feel, or behave based on what I am going to say?

Conscious communication takes time and energy plus adopting a focus on someone other than self. So why do it if it is so much work? What are the benefits of communicating with your brain engaged rather than merely your emotions? How do these benefits sound: less conflict, less pain, more understanding, a sense of peace and love, more problems solved, greater respect, mended relationships with more harmony. They are all achievable if you are willing to work at using feedback effectively to engage in talk that matters.

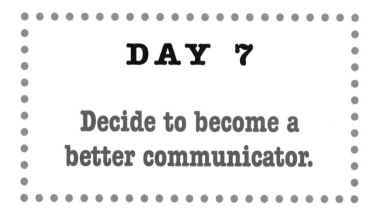

# DAY 7

## Decide to become a better communicator.

Committing yourself to being a better communicator means wanting to learn new skills and ways of relating to others. There is no silver bullet, no magic wand, only determination and hard work. "It is not a question of failing or of succeeding; it is simply a question of sticking to an idea until it becomes a tangible reality," wrote Ernest Holmes.[1] You choose to invest the time and energy that it will take to become a good communicator.

Remember, you did not learn your communication patterns overnight, and you won't fix them overnight. Since real change will take some time, consider your efforts and energy as investments that will bring you the positive relationships you want.

Returning to the mother-daughter telephone conversation in Day 6 (page 38), see what a difference feedback and communication adjustments can make. The following present two different approaches to the conversation. In the first one, Betsy adjusts her feedback to her mother's approach. And in the second conversation, her mother revises her feedback to better match Betsy's approach.

# Conversation 1

**Mother**: Betsy, you really should stop smoking. I've just read another article about the hazards of cigarette smoking. It talked about the negative effects that smoking has on women with Crohn's disease. And with your condition, you're putting yourself at risk. You're going to kill yourself before you're fifty and leave your husband and son to fend for themselves. How can you do that to people you love?

**Betsy**: Thanks for your concern, Mom. I'd be interested in reading the article. Would you send it to me?

**Mother**: Sure, I'll put it in the mail today. Smoking will kill you, but you seem to refuse to do anything about it.

**Betsy**: I know smoking is a bad habit and that I need to stop. I just need to find a way to do it so I don't gain twenty pounds, which is what happened the last time I tried to quit. I don't want that to happen again. The weight was too hard to lose. So, knowing my sensitivity about the weight, and with all your reading and knowledge on the subject, what approaches do you think might work for me?

What changes did Betsy make? She did a number of things differently. First, she did not react to the parental tone and use of the emotionally laden word *should*. *Should* is a hot button for many people and can raise the hair on the back of their necks. Few of us like to be told what we *should* do.

Second, Betsy did not answer the question her mother posed. Instead, she picked up on her mother's underlying concern for Betsy's well-being and consciously responded to a nonemotional item, the article her mother mentioned.

Third, when her mother pressed her on the smoking issue, rather than getting defensive or going on the offensive, Betsy agreed with her, taking the wind out of her mother's argument. And most importantly, Betsy got her mother to participate in solving her smoking problem. She did this by asking her mother an open-ended question. In a later principle, we will spend time talking about the importance of questions.

In this situation, the open-ended question drew Betsy's mother in rather than shut her out. The unspoken sentiment was, "You're smart. I appreciate your interest and information, and I want your help." Who wouldn't feel complimented?

> Consider your efforts and energy as investments that will bring you the positive relationships you want.

## Conversation 2

**Mother**: Betsy, how are you, dear?

**Betsy**: Fine, Mom. What's up?

**Mother**: Well, I was thinking about you as I was reading this article on the hazards of cigarette smoking because it talked about the negative effects that smoking has on women with Crohn's disease. It was the first article I'd seen on the subject, and it really scared me. If I had Crohn's and was a smoker, after reading that article, I'd quit immediately.

**Betsy**: Oh, Mother, for heaven's sake, don't be such a drama queen.

**Mother**: I'll put the article in the mail to you today so you can read it and judge for yourself. I know when you tried before to quit that you gained a lot of weight, and I recall how upset you were. I applaud you for your effort. I love you so much that I'd like to help you figure out an effective way to quit smoking so that you won't put on weight. What can I do to help you figure out a way?

Betsy's mother did several things right. First, she was honest about why she was calling and did not hide her feelings. She told Betsy about the article she had read. She did not judge her daughter. She talked about her fears for her.

Second, her mother did not overreact to Betsy's calling her a drama queen. By ignoring it she avoided getting dragged into a name-calling contest.

And, third, her mother complimented Betsy and gave her credit for trying to quit. From there, she built on this positive affirmation and offered Betsy help by using an open-ended question to engage them both in Betsy's problem-solving process.

Today, you have **two assignments**:

1. Assess how committed you are to improving your communication skills. Go back to "My Commitment to Listen to Others" in Day 3 (page 25). Based on what you have learned in the first seven days, pick a level that represents where you are now.

2. Write out a conversation you've recently had that went poorly. For example, "I said . . . He said . . . I said . . . He said . . ." Then, rewrite the conversation to see how you might change it and make it more effective.

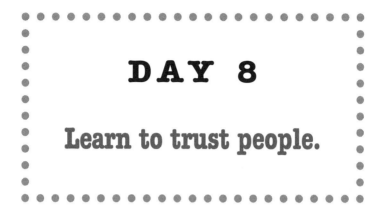

# DAY 8

## Learn to trust people.

The eighth principle requires you to take a risk. In talk that matters, trust and risk can be thought of as two sides of the same coin. On one side, if you trust someone, you are likely to take a risk with him or her. On the flip side, if you have taken a risk, it is probably because you trust the person. The two are intertwined. Without trust you cannot be totally honest with someone, and without risk you may appear aloof or guarded. So what creates trust?

Our definition of trust is *confident expectation*. Think about a person you trust. What is it about this person that holds your trust? What does he do or what does she say that makes you trust them? Quickly list the qualities that come to mind.

Did any of the following make your list?

- He does what he says he is going to do.
- She takes responsibility for her actions.
- He keeps his commitments to me.
- She tells me the truth.
- He doesn't blow up one day and then act sweet the next.
- I know what to expect.
- She lets me know what she expects of me.
- He keeps my confidences.
- She gives me a heads-up to possible trouble brewing.
- His behavior is consistent.

You might have listed some others as well. These actions and behaviors create trust in a relationship. When they exist, you have *confident expectations* of the other person.

Trust cannot be built overnight. It is a process of consistent, repeated actions demonstrated over a period of time. Additionally, trust cannot be bought. It is a unique gift—strong as steel, yet fragile as a snowflake.

Think about a time when someone you trusted broke that trust. How did you feel about that person afterward? Disappointed? Betrayed? Mad? Trust takes a long time to build and can be shattered with just one act. Take, for example, a ten-year marriage where a spouse strays. The strong trust developed over those ten years shatters like glass—and the confident expectations are gone.

Let's look at the other side of the coin—risk. Our definition of risk is *exposure to the chance of injury or loss.* In the marriage example, both partners went into the marriage trusting the marriage would last forever but with the *risk* that it might not.

With one partner injured, the dilemma for this person is whether to risk trying to fix the marriage. If you were in this situation, would you risk rebuilding trust? Or is that too risky?

First of all, what is *too* risky? Some persons deem an action too risky if it is physical, like reality show stunts of eating insects, walking on glass shards, and jumping out of airplanes. For others, what is too risky is an emotional event, as in confronting a spouse about having an affair. Each one of us defines what is too risky.

Some folks are more comfortable taking risks than others, which is why reality shows have contestants. There is no right or wrong in how much risk we are willing to take. It differs from person to person because we all have different tolerance levels. The goal is to understand our level of tolerance and then learn how to deal with what we feel is too risky for us.

> There is no right or wrong in how much risk we are willing to take. It differs from person to person.

How do you approach a situation that you feel is too risky? You may choose to deny, ignore, avoid, or dismiss it. You convince yourself that it is not happening or that it is not a problem. You may even persuade yourself that you can live with it.

In the marriage example, the injured party may say, "I can live with this. If I ignore the situation, eventually it will just go away." This option does not get to the root cause and solve the problem. Without addressing the issue, you are, in effect, condoning the behavior.

In contrast, you could blow up at your spouse and emotionally purge your system. This option may initially make you feel better. You may say, "How could you do this to me? I thought we were happy. How could you sneak around behind my back and hurt me like this? Pack your bags and get out! I hate you!" Again, this option will not solve the problem; in fact, it may make it worse.

When you face an issue that you feel may be too risky, stop, clear your mind, and ask yourself, *Why do I feel this way? What underlying fear am I facing? Is it the unknown? rejection? failure? embarrassment? loneliness? physical, mental, or emotional pain? Maybe even death?*

Whatever it is, identify it, and then ask yourself, *What's the worst thing that could possibly happen to me?* In our hypothetical example, the fear is probably a combination of most of the fears mentioned above, except for death. Emotional and mental pain plus embarrassment may be the greatest fears. Once you have identified and articulated the fear(s), and accepted the possible consequences, the next step is to confront the situation—in this case, your spouse.

So you engage in an approach called ***expectation-observation***. This technique allows you to risk and trust. It is part of a successful problem-solving process copyrighted by Interact Performance Systems, Inc., a management training company.[1] It works like this. You first state an *expectation*: "When we got married ten years ago, we made a vow to each other and agreed that we would be together for the rest of our lives." This reminds your spouse of your agreement and mutual expectations.

Next, you state an *observation*: "With this affair, that vow has been broken." You state that something has drastically impacted the original agreement and that you are concerned about it.

Then you *stop, pause*, and *wait* for a response. You want to hear what your spouse has to say about your observation. Pausing forces you to listen and offers your spouse the opportunity to speak.

As you listen, if you need more clarification say, "I'm not sure I understand what the problem is. Help me understand what's wrong." Then, stop and carefully listen. If appropriate, you may also reflect your spouse's feelings. For example, you might say, "It sounds like you're feeling trapped in our relationship."

Talk until you hear each other out and jointly come to a plan of action that you both can live with and support. It may not be the final solution to the problem, but it brings some closure to the current conflict and permits you both to move on in the relationship.

Here are some other situations that may be considered risky. For practice, apply the expectation-observation technique to these examples:

1. You need to tell your boss that you do not want to take your next promotion, along with its three-year overseas assignment.

   Expectation:

   Observation:

2. You need to tell your spouse that you are not having sex frequently enough to suit you, and you want more.

   Expectation:

   Observation:

3. You and your boss have argued; he has blown up at you, using abusive language. You need to tell him that you do not want to be treated in such a demeaning way.

Expectation:



Observation:



4  You need to tell an aging parent that due to her health and the attention she requires, she must move from your home.

Expectation:



Observation:



●   ●   ●


Today use the expectation-observation technique with two people—one person at work and one person at home—and engage in talk that matters to you.

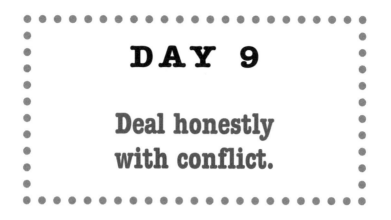

# DAY 9

## Deal honestly with conflict.

Communicating usually is hard work, especially when there is conflict in a relationship. Most of us feel anxious with conflict, and we choose either to fight back with words or to take flight into silence and fume. Early on we learn one of these two reactions to conflict and then perfect it for the rest of our lives. But does either fight or flight lead to a successful resolution of conflict and result in talk that matters? Let's look at an example of how the *fight* reaction to conflict can play out.

Tom and two of his buddies drop by their favorite bar for a few beers after work. Before they realize it, three hours have passed.

At 9:30 p.m., Tom arrives at home and walks through the front door. "Hello, dear!" he says.

"Where in the hell have you been?" his wife, Ellen, asks.

"I just had a couple of beers with the guys after work."

"How many times have I told you to call if you are going to be late for dinner?"

"I got caught up in the conversation and . . ."

"No more excuses!" Ellen says. "I'm tired of your self-centeredness and thoughtlessness and the way you never consider my feelings!"

At this point Tom has three choices: fight with words, retreat into silence, or talk in ways that matter.

## Option One—Fight with Words

Tom fights back with, "Sick and tired, huh? Who wants to rush home to a woman like you when all you do is bitch and moan about my measly salary and how much less I make than everyone else?"

When Tom turns on Ellen, they have lost any chance at meaningful talk. The harangue can go on for hours, and they will never come close to an understanding or resolution. If Tom and Ellen had recorded their conversation and listened to themselves, they would have recognized some old, familiar patterns. After an hour of battle, they may stop fighting out of sheer exhaustion; but they will be no closer to resolution. The arguing, blaming, and shouting at each other might vent their anger, but it will not create a resolution.

When Tom and Ellen encounter each other this way, the relationship is broken, and meaningful talk comes to a halt. Tom has been inconsiderate, but he does not admit it. Ellen responds with anger and blames Tom for his behavior. In turn, he offers weak excuses but no apology. Ellen punishes Tom with more anger and accusations.

Accusing, blaming, and discounting leave deep scars in the memory; the resulting pain often never completely goes away. It remains and simmers in the emotions until the next negative encounter. Can you imagine the accumulated pain from living with a spouse, working for a boss, or relating to a coworker like Tom or Ellen?

Now let's see how the *flight* reaction to conflict can look.

## Option Two—Retreat into Silence

When Ellen reprimands Tom for being late, he retreats into silence. He goes into the family room, turns on the TV, and picks up the newspaper.

Turning on the television symbolically says, "I'm not listening to you." The newspaper in front of his face says, "I'm not here, and I'm not available to you." Ellen's attack on Tom and Tom's retreat from Ellen widens the gap between them.

In the brief encounter with Ellen, Tom withdrew in three ways:

1.  He withdrew mentally from the conversation. His thinking shut down before he reacted to her attack. This wasn't a conscious, thoughtful, studied response but rather a patterned reaction he copied from similar situations when he found himself in conflict.

2.  He withdrew emotionally. He did not take the time to hear Ellen's true feelings. To get to that level of talk would have required that he ask a few questions, listen, take responsibility for his thought-lessness, and get beneath the anger. But he did not do that.

3.  He withdrew physically by going into the den, switching on the television, and hiding behind the newspaper.

Many of us feel anxious in conflicted relations, and the uneasiness deepens if the other person attacks and blames us. As children, some of us found safety by withdrawing from the conflict: "If I run away, they can't find me and hurt me." Neither fight nor flight generates talk that matters for Tom and Ellen—they miss the chance to resolve their conflict and restore a fulfilling relationship.

Finally, let's see how option three, talk that matters, works.

## Option Three—Talk That Matters

Meaningful talk begins with listening. Tom must listen to Ellen's "Where in the hell have you been" outburst and respond to her rather than react. What a difference it would have made if Tom had said, "I was thoughtless and inconsiderate of you. You have a right to be angry." And what if he had given her a chance to express her fear, frustration, and anger without defending his thoughtless behavior? If Tom cares about nurturing their relationship, he could promise to keep Ellen informed in the future and change his behavior by calling when he is going to be late.

Withdrawing mentally, emotionally, and physically destroys any possibility of talk that matters. Meaningful talk requires that both parties be engaged. When you find yourself in a conflicted situation, use the following three questions to help defuse the conflict:

1. *"What's wrong?"* Ask *that* question and be prepared to listen. If Tom had asked that question, Ellen would have said angrily, "You stopped off to drink with the guys, and I had no idea where you were."

Notice how conversation can proceed when one person listens and is willing to accept responsibility for a poor choice or a thoughtless action?

2. *"What are you feeling?"* Emotions are driving this conversation. If you know what the emotions are, you can deal with them honestly and not disguise them with anger and blame.

Tom could have said, "You felt angry that I didn't call."

"Yes."

"You had reason to be angry because I've done the same thing before. You probably felt like I didn't care."

"That too."

Once the emotional vein is opened, it may bleed more feelings; tempers will have to cool before a positive exchange can take place.

3. *"What can I do?"* Does Ellen want an apology? Does she want a promise that it will not happen again? Does she want a husband who is sensitive to her needs? Normally, the angry one wants to be heard and

taken seriously. Also, there needs to be a resolution and a plan to discourage the troublesome behavior in the future.

Making an effort to explore feelings and to resolve issues communicates a positive message to the offended person. Taking these actions says the following:

- "I care about our relationship, and I want to strengthen it."
- "I am strong enough to hear your criticism and anger and stay in the relationship without running away."
- "I am showing a degree of maturity by refusing to get in the blaming game and by giving you an opportunity to vent your feelings."

Option three, talk that matters, brings a rich payoff: a salvaged marriage, a renewed friendship, a healthier work environment, or even a deepened self-worth.

How often do you choose option three in a conflict situation? If you say "never" or "I don't know," take a minute and think about a recent conflict you handled badly. Now, replay the situation and instead of reacting as you did, insert the three questions. Then listen, and respond positively.

•    •    •

Today when a conflict situation arises and you are under attack, take a deep breath and ask the three questions of option three:

1. What's wrong?
2. What are you feeling?
3. What can I do?

When you ask these three questions and take positive action, you'll be closer to talk that matters and a healthy resolution to the conflict.

# TIME OUT

## Review your progress.

At this point in your study, you have

- begun to discover where you are in the art of talk that matters;
- made efforts to send a message about yourself to another;
- committed yourself to be an attentive listener;
- learned the rules for being a good listener;
- noted the importance of feedback;
- experienced some of the benefits of feedback;
- seen the power of trust in a relationship;
- recognized an effective way to deal honestly with conflict.

If you are still fuzzy about your ability to communicate effectively, review Day 1. Be honest with yourself about your ability to create and maintain a good relationship with a friend, spouse, supervisor, or new acquaintance.

If you have not fully developed the habit of speaking clearly about your values, needs, and dreams, don't go further until you review Day 2 and practice what you learn.

If you find yourself thinking about what you want to say when another is talking, you are not listening attentively. In positive relationships, listening is more important than speaking. Take your cue from Day 3, and commit yourself anew to the task.

If you have not mastered all the rules for effective listening, commit yourself to practice a new skill each day until you develop the reputation of being a good listener.

If you are confused about feedback, review Day 6. During the time you are speaking and even after you have finished, the feedback of the other person tells you whether you got your message across. Pay attention to the information that people send back to you.

If you are anxious about making the changes you are discovering, Day 8 will help you assess the degree of risk you can handle. All change demands risk. If you fear conflict and permit it to make you withdraw from a relationship, you will sacrifice your self-worth and your role in a relationship. Keep working on the insights in Day 8 until you are able to work through a tense encounter.

# DAY 10

## Talk straight.

Straight talk is saying what you honestly think and feel while respecting the feelings and opinions of others. Nothing blocks meaningful talk more than those who artfully dodge themselves and never own up to their ideas. These folks speak about what other people think and what statistics reveal, or they engage in vague theoretical arguments. They seldom say what they personally think or feel. As a result, when you grasp to understand their messages, they vanish like wispy vapors.

Cary, a mild-mannered architect, talked straight. He spoke of his ideas, thoughts, and wishes. He willingly shared his feelings about people or situations. In conversations with friends, he spoke from within himself. When asked to teach or lead, he spoke that way too. This man had no fear of others' judgments and required no one's approval. His vulnerability was totally disarming. An acquaintance of his, an accurate judge of human nature, once said, "Cary speaks from the place where words come from."

Speaking from "where words come from" prevents artful dodging and slick cover-ups and allows words from the heart and soul to emerge. These words express who you are, what you think, as well as where you stand. Sounds easy enough. But when you speak without covering up, you expose yourself to big risks, especially the risk that many of us fear most—rejection.

Sending messages that do not expose you seems to be safe. If people do not know who or what you are, they can't criticize or reject you. But if you choose to hide behind words that never show who you are, what do you gain? If you keep hiding, you stand to lose the self you were meant to be.

This hiding behavior is quite common. Think of the people in your life who skillfully hide their opinions, hopes, and desires. You can hear it in the conversation of an academic whose talk focuses on opinions and positions of authorities. You can spot it in the manager who has plenty to tell you about your performance or lack thereof but not too much about her needs or struggles.

Parents often find it difficult to admit to their children that they have no idea how to handle a sticky situation. Instead of admitting ignorance, a parent may say, "You're old enough to know how to handle this situation."

Often, we withhold our deepest needs from another, secretly hoping those needs will be noticed without being spoken. For example, instead of stating her desire to go out to dinner, a woman says to her husband, "Have you ever noticed how Jim and Frances go out to dinner every week?" Or, when you ask a friend who is in the middle of a divorce how things are going, rather than tell you his feelings, he says that everything is fine.

Talk that matters can only happen when people begin to speak honestly about themselves—their opinions, insights, needs, wants, and hopes. If you suspect you may be avoiding the expression of your feelings and thoughts, pay close attention to the way you answer questions and express opinions.

Here is an example of straight talk or talk from the inside. Julie and Tom are discussing dinner plans.

Julie asks, "What would you like to do about dinner tonight?"

Tom answers, "We could either go out or cook together at home."

"Okay, but what do you want to do?" Julie asks.

Tom replies, "I'd rather eat at home, but maybe you'd rather not cook."

"No, I've thought about it. I know that you've had a hard day, so let's eat in," says Julie.

In this simple, direct exchange both Tom and Julie are speaking clearly from the inside. But let's look at the same two people in another situation.

After dinner, Tom helps with the kitchen chores and when the last dish has been placed in the dishwasher, he and Julie sit down on the sofa to watch TV. After a few minutes of watching an old movie, Tom eases his arm around Julie.

> Only talk from the inside, straight talk, can clear the air.

"Did you notice the news broadcast that reported that couples our age have sex only once or twice a month?" Tom asks. She leans away from him.

"Yeah," Julie replies and then asks, "How did work go today?"

"Okay. Why do you think folks like us don't have sex more often?" asks Tom.

"Oh, I don't know," Julie answers. "Maybe they are busy, tired, or just not interested."

Tom displays frustration as he shifts his weight on the sofa, then says, "I don't think couples are disinterested. I don't think that at all. I think it's an unwillingness to give lovemaking a chance."

"I definitely believe the report. Some people don't need it!" Julie replies.

What's wrong with this conversation? How does it contrast with the former conversation about dinner? Why were they both skirting the issue of their sex life?

This conversation illustrates artful dodging. Tom and Julie know how to talk meaningfully, but this subject is emotion packed. In the past, they have had conflicts over their sex life, and previous efforts to discuss the matter ended in heated arguments and feelings of separation. Since neither of them wanted to touch off a conflict, they talked around the issue instead of openly stating their desires and feelings.

Sex is but one of numerous topics laden with emotional baggage. No matter what the subject—money, in-laws, religion, or sex—only talk from the inside, straight talk, can clear the air. How do people like Tom and Julie learn to speak from the inside about sensitive issues? Here are some actions that can help them and you speak from the inside:

- Identify your feelings (get in touch with your gut).
- Mentally put into words what you feel.
- State in "I" language your feelings, needs, desires, and wishes (I want . . . , I need . . . , I wish . . .).
- Leave room in your statements for another's needs and desires.
- Pay close attention to the other person's responses to you.
- Ask questions for further clarification.
- Avoid making judgments or issuing decrees.

This use of straight talk will result in resolution of the conflict if both parties want it. Here are some reasons why straight talk works:

- It is honest.
- It is vulnerable.
- It is believable.
- It honors the other person.
- It is open to receive and change.

- It leaves room for differences.
- It builds trust.

Straight talk from the inside works if both parties want to communicate and remove barriers. If either partner tries to control the outcome of the disagreement, communication will not work.

Not every encounter or conversation needs to have depth. You can acknowledge people without its leading to in-depth talk; for example, greeting an acquaintance with "How are you?" But if you want to have a significant encounter with another person, speak from the inside.

•   •   •

Try this simple exercise today. Notice how often other people in your life talk straight and from the heart. Assess your conversations on a scale from 1 to 5, 5 being meaningful and 1 being superficial.

*Conversation with neighbor this morning*

1    2    3    4    5

Then, analyze each conversation again to determine whether you talk straight or speak in clichés. Rate yourself on the same scale of 1 to 5.

# DAY 11

## Stand firm.

Simply put, standing firm means asserting yourself so you can be a partner in talk that matters. If you refuse to speak up or speak out, you will never be heard or understood. And if you express your feelings reluctantly, you will not connect with others.

Helena had worked for the same boss for more than thirty years. Dependable, she not only did her job well, she also took responsibility for her work. Her conversations with her boss about movies, current events, and job responsibilities flowed easily. But when the subject turned to Helena, she became quiet and withdrawn. In all the years that she worked for her boss, he never heard anything about her personal life. Helena was reserved and reluctant to talk about herself or her personal life. What might have triggered such reluctance?

- The culture she was reared in?
- The fear of being found out?

- The anxiety of being rejected?
- The fear of shame—being exposed in an embarrassing way?

To engage in dialogue, Helena needed to claim her own space and take part in the verbal exchange. We all need to define our own psychological and emotional space, the place where we can comfortably engage in communication with others. We must understand our thoughts and express ourselves honestly, clearly, and without apology. We have a right to be here. If we do not fill our space and offer our views and perceptions, our world will be a lesser place.

Where are you with this principle? Do you stand firm in the knowledge that your words are worthwhile? Are you open and talkative with close friends but quiet in the presence of someone you consider superior or assertive?

Let's look at Dan—the opposite of Helena's personality type, an egotistical boaster—and see what these two people may have in common when it comes to standing firm. Dan fills the air with words. He boasts of his successes, achievements, and relationships. His boasting can go on for hours; but as you listen, you learn little about the deeper dimensions of his life. Dan feigns greatness, but at some level you wonder if he actually believes in himself. His words might impress, but his self-worth is not firmly planted. If he were firmly grounded, he would not need to brag, to boast, or to impress. The ground beneath Dan's feet is actually quicksand—soupy, trembling, and shifting.

So what do these two people, Dan and Helena, have in common? On the surface, they appear to be opposites: the reticent woman hopes to be invisible, and the egotistical man is afraid that no one will notice him. Interestingly, they both suffer from the same dysfunction.

Both Dan and Helena need a clearly defined and valued self. It is not likely they will find that self until they recognize the inadequacy of their present behavior. The kind of self-discovery that will liberate them from their self-destructive patterns of behavior will require that they look within themselves to discover who they really are—their potential, their desires, and their inadequacies. As they begin to accept themselves, they will also begin to communicate from a more authentic position. This self-acceptance, however, can be tedious work, like peeling back the layers of an onion or putting together a thousand-piece jigsaw puzzle.

Within many of us there seem to be three persons desperately struggling with one another. First, there is the person we wish we were, an idealized but likely unreal self. Second, there is another person we fear that we are; this is a person whom we despise because he or she constantly undermines our idealized self. Third, there is a strong likelihood that we are neither of these false selves but a mixture of the two.

The different images of the self explain Dan and Helena's lack of grounding. Helena identifies with her despised self and uses silence to hide this unacceptable image. *If I don't reveal myself, people can't reject me,* she thinks. Dan presents an ideal self that reaches far beyond actuality. Fearful that the self he aspires to be will not be seen, he paints it large so that no one will miss it.

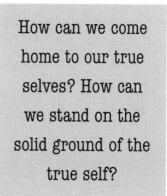

How can we come home to our true selves? How can we stand on the solid ground of the true self?

What both need is a solid real self. A good sense of who they are will give them firm ground to stand on and a place to speak from. How can we come home to our true selves? How can we stand on the solid ground of the true self? Here are some pointers:

1. You are neither your despised self nor your ideal self. This is both good news and bad news. The good news is that you are not a despised self to be hidden and feared. The bad news is that you are not the ideal self you wish you were. Yet, it is good news that to be accepted, valued, and important, you do not have to be that unreal, idealized self. You can be who you are!

2. You are a self that has worth, simply because you are. You have nothing in your essential being that you need to fear; therefore, you don't have to inflate a false image of yourself that you could never achieve.

3. Begin to discover who your real self is today. Use the way that you present yourself as an entry into finding your true self.

4. Notice how you talk with others. Are you quiet and reserved? Do you feel anxious when you speak? Is it difficult to express yourself? In the moment, what do you feel about yourself? Or, when you speak to others do you feel a need to impress them? Do you hear yourself dropping names of significant people? Do you frequently turn the conversation toward yourself? How do you react to people who do not confirm your superstar status?

5. Spend time reflecting on the data you uncover when you ask these hard questions. Your answers may lead you to change some of the ways you encounter others.

6. Speak from your true self. When you speak from your true self, your talk will increasingly be real talk, talk that matters. Paying attention to your current way of relating to others will open wide the door for solid self-talk.

   • Speak what you honestly think about a given topic. You will soon come home to your true self.

   • When you express honest feelings about a particular issue, you will experience your true self in action.

   • Whenever you resist the urge to hide your thoughts or feelings, you strengthen your true, expressive self.

   • When you avoid boasting, like reporting the important people you know and the exotic places you have visited, you will make space for conversation that is mutually enhancing.

- When self-awareness of how you speak begins to subside and your grounded, true-self conversation comes naturally, you are getting to be at home with yourself.

•   •   •

Here is an exercise for today. Observe your talk with friends, associates, and strangers; pay attention to how often you talk from your *real* self, your *ideal* self, and your *despised* self.

Make a few notes about your observations during the day. Review them in the evening or the next morning. Try not to judge or evaluate yourself negatively. When you care enough to notice and review your life, change has already begun.

# DAY 12

## Help others (and yourself) speak up.

The twelfth principle invites you to help others speak up, to express their ideas, opinions, and desires. It is hard to connect with others who continually give in and don't assert themselves. When they don't speak up, they sacrifice their power, often making them feel helpless. When they give up their place and fail to assert themselves, nobody knows where they stand or even who they really are. Interaction with these people is like talking to a statue.

Did you ever wonder what was going on with such a reticent person? Often people who continually withhold their thoughts and desires

- don't feel good about themselves;
- see others as better;
- think others know more;
- judge themselves as never getting it right;
- have great difficulty accepting affirmation.

Can you help friends or employees develop a mind of their own, find their own voice, and stand up for what they believe? Although you cannot fix the person, here are three things that you can do to create an environment that encourages others to speak up:

## Create space

People who struggle with self-esteem often need both physical and emotional space. You can create physical space by honoring an appropriate distance between you and the other person. When people back away, they indicate that you have invaded their safety zone; so give them room. Additionally, you can create emotional space with words of empathy and assurance, as the following story illustrates.

Emily works in a grocery checkout line. John is her manager. For several days Emily has been unusually slow checking out customers. John dreads giving her needed constructive criticism because her passivity makes conversation difficult.

John approaches her at the cash register. As soon as she sees him, she backs up against the register. Her backing away signals John to yield some ground if he wants to hear what she has to say.

So John backs up and then says, "Emily, your line has been getting longer and longer. We need to move things along more quickly."

At this point, Emily drops her head, looks at the floor, and replies, "I've not been feeling well the past few days." Her voice is barely audible. Reading her nonverbal communication, John knows that he cannot continue until Emily feels more comfortable with the conversation.

John says, "Please come to my office so we can talk more freely." In the office, he motions for her to sit in the chair nearest the door. When she is seated, he continues, "I'm sorry that you haven't been feeling well, and I want to help you."

In this encounter, John makes space for Emily—physical space by seating her near the door and emotional space with words of assurance and empathy. He has begun to help her stand on her own feet and develop confidence.

## Encourage a voice

Help the passive person find a voice. Here are three statements a good communicator can use to help someone find his or her voice:

1. Ask for his or her opinions: "What do you think about the idea?"
2. Respond positively to his or her insights: "What a good idea!"
3. Give credit for his or her good choices: "That really makes sense. Good choice."

Each of these statements can help a reticent communicator speak more freely. You give energy when you help a person speak his or her mind, as the following example shows.

Bill was a trained teacher, but he felt unsure of himself. In personal conversations he spoke freely and clearly, but when he stood up before a group, he swallowed his voice. He opened his mouth and moved his lips, but the words came out muffled and with an air of apology. He had never found his own voice.

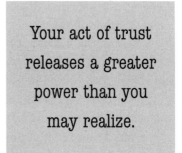

Your act of trust releases a greater power than you may realize.

In one of his early assignments, he worked with Jennifer, who had been a teacher and public speaker for three decades. They worked together in the classroom, with Jennifer as the lead teacher and Bill as the assistant. When Bill occasionally substituted for Jennifer, his voice was weak. After seeing his struggle, Jennifer suggested that he had a great deal to say and that he should trust himself more fully in his speech. In a few months, his presentations got stronger. His voice became clearer, and he began to express deep conviction about the subject he taught. From time to time, Jennifer spoke positively of his changes, and he smiled and nodded with gratitude. The strength of Bill's voice became evident not only in lectures and friendly conversations but also in faculty meetings and committee meetings.

## Trust the changes

Trust the changes that you see in passive people who begin to speak up and stand up for themselves. Your act of trust releases a greater power than you may realize. As long as you see the person as passive, retiring, or even inept, you tend to lock him or her into that role. The image becomes a self-fulfilling prophecy. But when you affirm changes and give more responsibility and trust to passive people, they often begin to measure up to your expectations. Your expectations enable them to change.

Maybe you are the one who feels ill at ease with others, especially those you do not know. Or, perhaps when even a friend or spouse invades your space you feel anxious and unable to speak and interact freely. So what might you do? The answer differs slightly from what we have suggested you do for others. You can

- *Claim your space.* When anyone gets too close for comfort, ask for more space. State your discomfort. Move away. If someone invades your emotional space, use the same approach.
- *Believe in yourself.* You have value. Be a good friend or a loving companion. Believing in your worth will strengthen your voice. Self-confidence will help you project your words and your feelings.

At first, claiming your worth and expressing yourself will feel strange. If you have never believed that you have a place in the world and a right to express yourself, beginning to exercise this freedom will open a whole new way of being for you. Get ready for energy and excitement as you discover new ways of expressing the person you truly are. As you begin to express yourself:

- *Trust your heart.* As you discover what you think, feel, and desire, trust yourself. You may have spent so much of your life trying to please others that you've never asked what would most please you. From time to time, you will be tempted to slip back into your old way of seeing yourself and seeking others' approval. Don't do it!

- *Catch yourself.* Notice the first onslaught of anxiety. Generally, anxious feelings come before negative thoughts like *What will others think of me? What do they expect of me?* Pay attention to your feelings and identify them. Sometimes, however, anxiety begins with negative, fearful, self-depreciating thoughts. The moment you surrender to either your negative thoughts or anxious feelings, your desire to speak up will falter.

- *Keep your power.* Negative thinking and anxiety can lead you to give your power away. Staying in touch with yourself and your worth gives you tremendous power. You are equal to any other human being anywhere. You have a right to be here. Every anxious thought and every question about your worth erodes this power. When you fear another, you give that person power over you. When you need another's approval or affirmation, you give that person power over you. Don't give away your power!

●　　●　　●

Today as you stand confidently and speak up, remember others in your sphere of influence. Encourage someone's voice today. Choose someone who is reticent to speak up, then (1) Ask for his or her opinion. (2) Respond positively to his or her insights. (3) Give that person credit for his or her good choices.

Helping them speak up will help you too!

# DAY 13

## Build partnerships.

**T**alk that matters requires a partnership of speaker and listener. This joint venture involves two people who want to communicate more than they want to control the outcome of the encounter. Anything less than a partnership can lead to manipulation, game playing, and egotism, all causes of failed communication and, ultimately, failed relationships.

You will find that partnerships work in every kind of relationship. For example, Holly and Christy have been friends since grammar school. Their relationship spans kindergarten through college, marriage, and parenthood. One reason this friendship lasted through a myriad of changes is both women's desire to keep the relationship alive through differences and misunderstandings. When Holly had not heard from Christy for six months, Holly called her and asked what had happened. The simple call opened the way for Christy to confess her neglect and add that nothing was amiss. A partnership works when both value the relationship, as these women do.

Partnerships also work in marriages. Eric and Melissa have been married for eight years. Both have been married before and both previous marriages ended in divorce. From those painful experiences they learned that forming a partnership worked better than pressing for their own way in family decisions. For example, early in the marriage, Melissa's two kids asked Eric for permission to go swimming, and he said okay. When Melissa learned that Eric had given the kids permission to go swimming just before dinner, she said to them in Eric's presence, "You can't go swimming now. It's time to eat dinner."

After dinner Eric said to Melissa, "If you want to rear the children by yourself, I'm okay with that; but if you want my help, you can't undermine my decisions, especially in front of the kids." Melissa recognized that for two years as a single mom she had made all the decisions regarding the children. She also recognized that her overruling Eric's decision told the children that she did not trust his judgment. When confronted with the choice Eric offered, Melissa told him, "I want parenting to be a joint venture." She never overruled Eric again. Partnerships can be maintained by resolving differences as they occur.

Partnerships work in business but not like the following example. Sarah works for a management consulting firm. For one year she had an engagement with a multibillion-dollar soft-drink conglomerate. Because of mergers and acquisitions and the need to upgrade the firm's systems, her analysis and recommendations had been extensive. After completing this internal work, Sarah's company made a proposal to the conglomerate for the work that needed to be done.

The project was approved at all the lower levels, but because it was several million dollars, it also required board approval. The board gave its approval. But even with board approval, the people Sarah had been working with for a year began to back off the deal. They claimed the price was too high and that the need was not as great as Sarah insisted. Instead, they suggested that they might need another bid.

This hesitation on the part of the firm seemed to Sarah and her associates a ploy for cutting the price. What would you call this move? Game playing? Manipulation? Or is it more malicious?

The firm's response seems to indicate no partnership with Sarah's company. For twelve months, teams worked together to discover what the company needed and how to proceed in correcting procedures. But after the preliminary work was done, the company's management tried to stiff-arm the consulting firm. These tactics violated all the basic rules of partnership. Trust must exist if dealings are to be amicable and not combative.

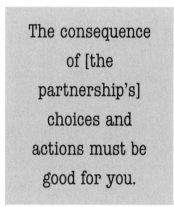

The consequence of [the partnership's] choices and actions must be good for you.

What does it take to achieve partnership between two individuals? Here are three essential ingredients:

First, the partnership must be good for you. When we have decided on a direction and have begun to achieve our goal, the consequence of our choices and actions must be good for you. This means that the decision meets your needs, rewards you, and honors you.

Second, the partnership must be good for me. Our decision also must meet my needs, reward me, and honor me.

Third, both our goals must be realized. To sacrifice achievement for the sake of feeling good toward each other undermines the aims of partnership. In friendship, marriage, and business, successful partners must agree on goals. Both Holly and Christy wanted their friendship to deepen and continue. Both Eric and Melissa wanted harmony and a shared authority in rearing their children. But the soft-drink conglomerate and Sarah's consultant firm did not seem to have mutually agreed-upon goals. Unstated conflicting goals weaken the partnership. To avoid this erosion, the partners begin by stating their goals openly, being prepared to negotiate, and communicating until they agree on a shared goal.

Think about a partnership in which you are successfully engaged. Who is involved in the partnership? How did it begin? How much do you value it? In the list of words below circle all the words that apply to this successful partnership.

| | | | |
|---|---|---|---|
| Open | Result-centered | Short-term | Sincere |
| Responsible | Trusting | Win/Lose | Shared |
| Manipulative | Controlling | Deceptive | Selfish |
| Competitive | Valued | Win/Win | Successful |
| Lasting | Honest | Person-centered | Caring |

Now, think about a partnership that has not been as successful. Place a check mark by the words that seem to apply to that broken relationship. Next, look at the relationship from the standpoint of the three essential ingredients: good for you, good for me, and achieves the goal. Where did it fail? How might the partnership be salvaged?

●　　●　　●

Your assignment today is to choose one constructive act you believe might help restore a broken relationship and to act on it. For example, you might ask for forgiveness, reveal more of yourself, be honest in your feelings, avoid imposing guilt, ask how the other is feeling, or ask for help. Look back over the previous principles for some additional ideas.

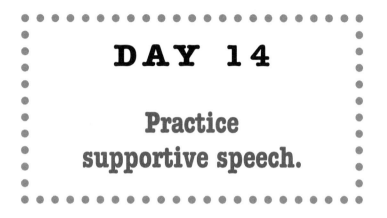

# DAY 14

## Practice supportive speech.

**E**very significant relationship in life thrives on supportive talk—talk that is genuine, caring, and encouraging. The suggestions we make in this principle will help you practice supportive talk in all your relationships, whether it is a friend who has been jilted by her lover, a family member who has been told he has terminal cancer, a neighbor whose child has been arrested for drug possession, or a colleague who has just been fired. Talk that matters in all these conditions is essential to the one who is struggling.

When you encounter situations such as these, do you feel helpless to say or do the right thing? Do you find yourself overcome with feelings of fear, a sense of utter loss, hopelessness, or even disappointment? How can you be of help? What can you say that will matter?

Michael's mentor, Warren, recently learned that he had pancreatic cancer. The doctor's prognosis was that Warren had six months to live. When Michael learned about Warren's plight, he prepared to visit Warren.

As Michael drove to Warren's house, he remembered all the things that Warren had meant to him. For ten years Warren walked with him through a painful marriage; he had been a friend during the divorce and its aftermath; he had been available to Michael's children when they struggled with accepting that painful experience; and he had taught Michael to know himself and become a more authentic person.

When Michael entered the house, he greeted the family members who were present. Warren lay on the couch propped up on a pillow. Michael walked over to the couch, knelt down, and warmly hugged Warren. He then took a chair and asked, "How are you?" He listened as Warren told him about the symptoms, the surgery, and his decision not to have extended treatment.

After listening for a long time, Michael knew that it was time to leave. As he was getting ready to leave, he said, "You know, Warren, you've changed my life. I'm a different person because of your influence and concern for me. Thank you. If you need me for anything, I'll be here for you." Without lingering, Michael departed with a heavy heart.

How can you be as supportive to the people in your life as Michael was to Warren in this visit? It is best to begin with a few suggestions about what *not* to do. For example, don't try to fix people who are in unbearable pain. If an easy solution to their pain exists, they already would have thought of it. They ache deeply, and there often is no immediate or effective anesthetic.

Also, don't try to explain the situation or the pain. Many times, there is no explanation. Platitudes such as "God has reasons that we don't understand" offer little help. The promise that "one day you'll see a reason for this" provides no consolation in the midst of personal agony.

When supporting a friend in pain, there are also words not to speak. When you are with someone who is suffering inexplicable grief, don't say, "I know what you're feeling." You don't! You may know what you felt when you faced a similar situation, but those were your feelings, not those of your friend. You can't truly know another's pain.

The most supportive action often is to say nothing. Sometimes the best talk is no talk. Instead, simply be present. Be silent. Compassionate feelings have a way of being communicated without words.

In a crisis like Warren's terminal illness, nothing you say or do will change the haunting facts. Admit your impotency, your humanness, and your own vulnerability to disastrous experiences in life. Permit yourself to feel the raw edges of your own humanity in the presence of another's inexplicable loss. These responses will shorten the distance between you and a suffering friend.

Simply being there often is the best you have to offer. A heartfelt touch—an arm around a shoulder or holding a hand—communicates more profoundly than any words. If you feel that you must speak, that you must put something into words, consider saying something like:

- "I am so sorry."
- "I love (or appreciate) you very much."
- "Can I do anything?"
- "I am available if you need me."
- "I can't imagine what it must be like."

● ● ●

Today remember a time when you were face-to-face with a person who was in enormous pain. What did you say or do? What do you think you might say or do now?

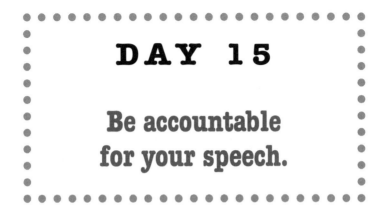

# DAY 15

## Be accountable for your speech.

If you seriously want to change and start engaging in talk that matters, then personal accountability to another for that change will play a part. Personal accountability is hard work, and we often avoid it. See if any of the following objections to accountability sound familiar:

Tom says, "I can handle my own changes; I don't need someone holding me accountable."

Dick reacts, "Accountability feels too much like having someone looking over your shoulder."

"Actually," Jane says, "I may want to back down on my decision; if another person knew of my failure, I'd feel embarrassed."

All these objections spring from a distorted idea of accountability. Making yourself accountable to another person does not mean you have a character flaw. And it does not mean that someone wants to rein you in or expose your weaknesses. A relationship of accountability involves trust and mutual interest that makes honesty easier and change possible.

Al had been the production manager in a food company for twenty years. In recent months, through a company-sponsored course in interpersonal communication, he became aware that he intimidated employees. During most of his managerial career he had used intimidation to discipline and control employees. The training session helped him realize that his harsh reprimands masked his own feelings of insecurity.

One person in the company knew about this disturbing problem better than anyone else—Maria, his secretary. Maria often witnessed Al's angry outbursts and his insensitive manner of correcting employees. She saw the terror on the faces of those who were called into his office and the mixture of pain and anger on their faces when they left. Many of them sought her advice and counsel, as did Al.

During the communication course, the trainer recommended that those who wanted to change their behavior become accountable to someone they trusted. Al recognized his insensitive actions. At first he uttered the expected, stereotypical responses—don't need it, don't like it, don't want to be embarrassed if I fail. As he continued to struggle with the challenge, he began to warm to the notion of accountability. He searched his mind for the one person that he could trust to help him.

> **A relationship of accountability involves trust and mutual interest that makes honesty easier and change possible.**

Whom could he turn to for help? Finally, he asked Maria if she would help him with his uncontrollable anger. He told her he wanted to become more positive and to build up people rather than tear them down.

Having asked Maria to help him be accountable, he stated specifically what he wanted from her. "Tell me what I do and say that intimidates people. I want to correct my actions."

The request took Maria aback. Could she offer feedback to her boss? Would he listen? Would she become the object of his anger if she told him the truth? Frankly, Maria was so shocked by Al's request that she asked him for some time to think about it.

As she considered Al's request, she decided to accept the challenge for the good of the company, for the morale of the employees, as well as for Al's personal growth. She decided to make a list of what she wanted to say to Al when she accepted his challenge. Here is what she wrote:

- Because I believe in you and in the value of this company, I will accept your challenge.
- In this relationship I must be free to act as a colleague and not as your employee.
- I will feed back to you what I see and hear regarding your treatment of people.
- What I say to you will be positive, constructive, and confidential.
- I will not embarrass you, nor will I tell anyone else in this company of my role.
- I would like you to consider this a verbal contract and count on me as a partner in this endeavor.

When she finished reading the statements, she gave a copy to Al. Al felt vulnerable, but he had set the wheels of change in motion; so, with Maria's help, he felt he could make changes in his life.

Deciding to make a change was not easy for Al, nor is it easy for any of us. Nevertheless, choosing a person who will be honest with us, support us, and struggle with us often spells the difference between success and failure. We are more likely to do what we have decided if we make ourselves accountable to another.

• • •

Today think about one person you trust enough to ask to hold you accountable while you are learning new skills in meaningful talk. Ask him or her for a commitment to help you, and together develop a plan of action.

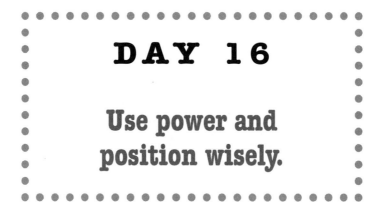

# DAY 16

## Use power and position wisely.

When you are in a position of power, how do you use that power? By power we mean the authority to give direction to the schedules of others, the influence to change circumstances, and the freedom to invite or reject people in your life. You may be in an authority role because you are a teacher, manager, parent, head of a committee or volunteer organization, or some other position of influence. Do you use your power for the benefit of those over whom you have control?

When used thoughtfully and sparingly, power or authority provides direction, order, and stability in a relationship or in a group. But when abused, authority becomes disruptive and destructive. Authority is like money in the bank—the less you use it, the more you have of it.

When you are in a role of authority, you cannot control how people you supervise see or feel toward you, but you can send signals that you are a friend rather than a foe. Consider the effects of the following behaviors:

- An administrator comes to work every day, enters her office, and closes the door. It remains closed all day.
- A father travels in his sales job all week and plays golf every weekend. He is seldom available to his teenage son.
- A wife ignores the advances of her husband, leaving him feeling undesirable and rejected.
- A budding love dries up because one of the friends is preoccupied with other responsibilities.
- A friendship runs aground because the more "successful" friend tends to advise and criticize her former partner.

Phil's behavior illustrates ways to correct the abuses implicit in the above examples. After he earned an MBA, Phil worked for a number of years for several large consulting firms. During that time, he observed executives and managers who often seemed distant, inaccessible, and intimidating. When he started his own business, Phil established a model of authority that might be called the AAA Quotient—a promise to be available, accessible, and accepting. This commitment has helped ease relationships between Phil and those who report to him.

Let's examine Phil's commitment. First, he agreed to be available to the people who work with him. His open-door policy speaks volumes to his employees. It says the boss is here; he is open to hear our problems and issues; and what goes on in this office matters to him. Contrast this message with that of the closed-door administrator mentioned above.

Second, Phil committed himself to be accessible to anyone in the company. He flattened the organization by removing layers of management between himself and the people who worked for him. He chose not to have an administrative assistant, and he denied other administrators in the company this luxury. From firsthand experience, Phil learned that administrative assistants can become gatekeepers who control accessibility to the boss. He eliminated that barrier both for himself and others. As a consequence of his availability and accessibility, employees often came to his office with reports and suggestions that gave him much-needed information and contributed to the company's success.

Third, Phil was committed to being an accepting person. He witnessed the devastating effects of managers chewing out subordinates, snubbing employees, and ignoring other managers. He neither took that approach nor allowed others in the company to behave that way. On one occasion, a call center employee gave incorrect information to a customer that cost the company several thousand dollars. Because she felt confident of Phil's acceptance, the employee walked into Phil's office and explained the situation to him instead of waiting for him to discover the mistake.

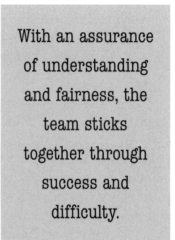

With an assurance of understanding and fairness, the team sticks together through success and difficulty.

Phil was unhappy about the mistake, but he did not punish the employee for her error. He did not dismiss her. Instead, he expressed his concern, explained how the matter could have been handled, and used the situation as a learning opportunity for both himself and the employee.

Aa a result of Phil's management policy, his team members work together to achieve challenging goals. With an assurance of understanding and fairness, the team sticks together through success and difficulty.

The company has prospered; its net worth has grown over a hundred times in twenty years. Phil's AAA Quotient—available, accessible, and accepting—has provided the structure for sharing information, group planning, and problem solving that has made the company a success.

The AAA Quotient worked in this business setting, and it will work in other settings as well. These include parent-child relationships, relationships with friends, and relationships between teachers and their students.

• • •

Do you want to be the kind of person who makes it easy for others to talk with you? If so, think about those who look to you for guidance. Today practice with them the AAA Quotient by being available, accessible, and accepting. Notice their reactions. What impact do the new behaviors have on your relationship with them?

**TIME OUT**

**Review your progress.**

**B**y the time you have reached this second review, you have learned

- to talk straight about your thoughts, feelings, and desires without hiding your true meanings. If you continually find yourself saying "some people" or "someone ought to" or if you often rely on sources outside the conversation, you are probably not sending a straight message. To work on this issue, review Day 10.

- to stand firm in your own space, claim your own voice, and speak your ideas forthrightly and clearly. If you discover that you frequently get queasy in a conversation, blame yourself for failures, and feel inferior in a relationship, review the suggestions in Day 11.

- to claim your power in a relationship. People who feel insecure in a relationship often ascribe to the other person powers that she or he does not have. If you discover that you are feeling uncertain about yourself, perceiving the other person as all powerful or at least more powerful than you, review the different approaches in Day 12.

- to keep relationships healthy and growing. If you find that valued relationships frequently become testy, if you notice that friends and associates avoid you, and if you find yourself willing to walk away from an important relationship, seek an answer in Day 13.

- to facilitate a positive conversation in a delicate situation. All of us experience occasions when we do not know the proper words to say. If you avoid difficult situations because you do not know what to say, Day 14 offers help.

- to enlist the help of a trusted friend to hold you accountable for your decision to become a better communicator. If you find yourself not following through on a decision to change, review Day 15.

- to use authority wisely. If you have been promoted to a new position or you are unsure how to use personal authority or influence well, review Day 16.

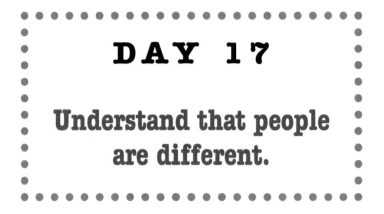

# DAY 17

## Understand that people are different.

No two of us are alike. We differ in our reactions, interests, values, motivations, skills, work habits, and ways we develop friendships, worship, vote, communicate, think, and see the world—just for starters.

What makes us different? One theory credits the nature-nurture balance. Fifty percent of our personality is determined by our genetic makeup, our nature. The other fifty percent is determined by our environment, the nurture of people who have influenced us and our individual experiences.

It is mind-boggling that of all the people in the world, no two of us are alike. But it makes sense when you think about the millions upon millions of combinations of genes and the variety of life experiences. The challenge for those who want to engage in talk that matters is figuring out how to communicate with all these different kinds of people.

One tool to help us understand differences among people is the Myers-Briggs Type Indicator® personality inventory, commonly referred to as the MBTI® assessment. This personality inventory was developed by an American mother-daughter team, Katharine Briggs and Isabel Briggs Myers. Their work, based on Jungian type theory, makes Carl Jung's ideas about perception, judgment, and attitudes useful in understanding ourselves and others.

Type theory suggests that what seems like random behavior is really not so random. The variation in our behavior is really orderly, consistent, and predictable because of our preferences for how we perceive things and how we come to conclusions about what we perceive.

The MBTI® assessment tool measures personality preferences. These preferences are similar to the preference each of us has for right- or left-handedness. We can use both hands, but we reach with our preferred hand first.

> **Type theory suggests that what seems like random behavior is really not so random.**

The MBTI® provides a useful measure of personality. It describes four dichotomies, each made up of a pair of opposite preferences. These four dichotomies can also be thought of as four activities. What follows are these four activities along with the pair of opposite preferences for each activity or dichotomy:

1. Energizing—where a person draws energy points to either a preference for Extraversion (E) or a preference for Introversion (I);

2. Perceiving—how a person takes in information points to either a preference for Sensing (S) or a preference for Intuition (N);

3. Deciding—how a person makes decisions points to either a preference for Thinking (T) or a preference for Feeling (F);

4. Living—the lifestyle a person adopts points to either a preference for Judging (J) or a preference for Perceiving (P).

All of the activities/dichotomies will be addressed individually in the next four chapters. What follows is an introductory description of each pair of preferences for each of the four activities/dichotomies. As you read through the various descriptions, think about which preference in each of the opposite pairs resonates with you.[1]

## Energizing

| Extraversion (E) | Introversion (I) |
|---|---|
| Preference for drawing energy from the outside world of people, activities, and things | Preference for drawing energy from one's internal world of ideas, emotions, and impressions |

## Perceiving

| Sensing (S) | Intuition (N) |
|---|---|
| Preference for taking in information through the five senses and noticing what is actual | Preference for taking in information through a "sixth sense" and noting what might be |

## Deciding

| Thinking (T) | Feeling (F) |
|---|---|
| Preference for organizing and structuring information to decide in a logical, objective way | Preference for organizing and structuring information to decide in a personal, values-oriented way |

| Judging (J) | Perceiving (P) |
|---|---|
| Preference for living a planned and organized life | Preference for living a spontaneous and flexible life |

Now that you've had a chance to read the descriptions for each pair of opposite preferences, circle the letter of the preference in each of the pairs that best describes you. Put the four letters together on the line below to form your "best guess" type.

## My "Best Guess" Type

___  ___  ___  ___

The only way to obtain your true type is by taking the MBTI® inventory. If you would like more information on taking the assessment, go to www.mbticomplete.com, or contact:

CPP, Inc.
1055 Joaquin Road, 2nd Floor
Mountain View, CA 94043
1-800-624-1765

To give you some context for your "best guess" type, here are the estimates of type distribution in the general United States population:

65–75 percent prefer Extraversion (E) to Introversion (I)
75 percent prefer Sensing (S) to Intuition (N)
67 percent of males prefer Thinking (T) to Feeling (F)
67 percent of females prefer Feeling (F) to Thinking (T)
55 percent prefer Judging (J) to Perceiving (P)[2]

If you assemble these preferences, you arrive at either a preference for ESTJ or ESFJ, depending upon gender, for the general United States population.[3] These are just two of sixteen possible types resulting from the variety of preference combinations. These sixteen types are displayed in the following Type Table.[4]

## TYPE TABLE

| ISTJ | ISFJ | INFJ | INTJ |
|------|------|------|------|
| ISTP | ISFP | INFP | INTP |
| ESTP | ESFP | ENFP | ENTP |
| ESTJ | ESFJ | ENFJ | ENTJ |

The Type Table is not designed to stereotype you or put you neatly into a little box. Rather, its purpose is to display the variety and combinations of preferences that exist among people. No type is better than another; all are of equal value.

You may be surprised to find that many of your friends will be in the same area of the Type Table as you and that you may have no acquaintances in some of the other types. To help you better engage in talk that matters with all types of people, you may want to seek out and learn more about people with a different type than your own.

•   •   •

Today spend fifteen minutes thinking about how your "best guess" type may impact those closest to you at work and at home. We'll revisit your "best guess" type later in the book after you've had a chance to immerse yourself in the concepts.

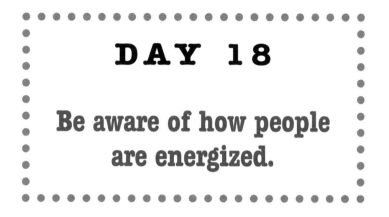

# DAY 18

## Be aware of how people are energized.

Understanding the source of another's energy can help you engage in talk that matters. Looking at MBTI® preferences, your energy preference will indicate whether you have a preference for Extraversion or Introversion. If your preference is Extraversion, you tend to draw your energy from the outside world of people, activities, and events. With an Extraversion preference, you probably enjoy parties, like to be on the go, engage in a lot of activity, and spend time with people.

With an Introversion preference, you tend to draw your energy from the inner world of your ideas and thoughts. With this preference, chances are you enjoy time alone and prefer more solitary activities like backpacking, surfing the net, or chess. You likely find cell phones intrusive.

To see this difference demonstrated, note how an Extraverted type and an Introverted type manage stress. Generally, an Extraverted type will turn to the outside world for relief. He may go to the mall, call a friend for lunch, or go to the gym. Extraverted types generally prefer an activity outside themselves that will stimulate and reenergize them.

On the other hand, an Introverted type who needs to release stress favors turning inward to find renewal. The Introverted type may pick up a good book she has been longing to read, practice yoga, or carve out some quiet time to listen to some favorite music. In general, Introverted types prefer to withdraw and go inside to recharge.

The difference in energy preference between the Extraverted and Introverted types can often result in communication conflicts. This occurs because each has different expectations of the other. The Extraverted type expects the Introverted type to communicate with energy and enthusiasm, responding quickly without long pauses to think. The Introverted type expects the Extraverted type to be quiet and thoughtful and allow time for reflection. What do you suppose happens when these two types meet? It could go something like this.

> The difference in energy preference between the Extraverted and Introverted type can often result in communication conflicts.

Josh, with a preference for Extraversion, enthusiastically greets Sharon and comments on the beautiful weather so unusual for this time of year. Sharon, an Introverted type, keeps her energy and enthusiasm inside and pauses before responding to Josh's comment. Expecting but not hearing a quick response, Josh asks Sharon a question to draw her out. Sharon, just getting ready to comment, now has to shift gears and decide how to answer his question. Josh, not hearing anything yet from Sharon, asks a second question. Sharon, feeling pressured that Josh is not allowing her enough time for a proper answer, becomes annoyed and confused about how to respond so focuses inward on her own thoughts and ignores Josh's comment and two questions.

So Josh poses a third question, convinced that enough questions will draw Sharon out. But he is mistaken. To Sharon, it's an annoyance; the barrage of questions feels like an interrogation that requires too much energy. To avoid this annoyance, Sharon retreats inside and makes no comment. Josh, expecting some witty repartee, gives up, and walks away thinking Sharon is dull and boring or worse—aloof. Sharon, with different expectations, vows to avoid this aggressive human being in the future.

Our energy preference can create conflict when we do not understand and respect each other's preferences. If Josh had simply backed off initially and allowed Sharon some space and time to respond to his weather comment, what do you suppose would have happened? Certainly the outcome would have been different; they might possibly have had a pleasant conversation.

•   •   •

Today think of two friends you believe may have a preference for Extraversion. What do they say and do that gives you the impression they may have this preference? Now think of two other friends you believe may have a preference for Introversion. What in their behaviors gives you the impression they may be Introverted types? Check the accuracy of your perceptions by asking each friend how he or she is energized. Then ask them to guess your energy preference and identify the behaviors that support their guess.

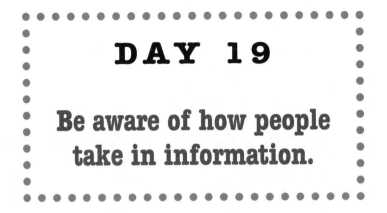

# DAY 19

## Be aware of how people take in information.

On this nineteenth day, we will look at the Sensing-Intuition dichotomy that is a preference for how people take in information about the world around them. Do you know how you perceive the world you're in?

If you take in information through your five senses (taste, touch, smell, sight, and sound), and notice what is tangible and concrete, you have a preference for Sensing. For example, consider an encounter with a salesperson. During a purchase, as a Sensing type, you probably can describe the salesperson's appearance, eye color, hairstyle, clothing, and other distinguishing characteristics—plus details of the transaction.

As a Sensing type, you probably like to do things with a practical bent; you like details, are comfortable when proceeding step-by-step, and seldom make factual errors. However, on the flip side, you may ignore your own inspirations.

If you take in information through a sense above and beyond the five senses and note what might be, you have a preference for Intuition. Let's return to the salesperson. With a preference for Intuition, you probably find yourself focusing not so much on the details of the transaction but rather on the bigger picture, wondering what kind of day he is having or where he is from or why he may be working at this particular store. If you like to do things with a creative bent, have a preference for the big picture, like proceeding in bursts of energy following your own inspirations, sometimes overlooking facts, then you may be an Intuitive type.

What impact does this preference have on your ability to engage in talk that matters? Although these preferences may not seem so different on the surface, the differences can be a source of misunderstanding and conflict. Let's see how conflict might arise.

Tyler, who has a preference for Sensing, wants to buy some ski wax for his brand new skis. He is in a hurry and pressed for time. Unaware that Joe is an Intuitive type, he asks Joe to assist him. Tyler describes his skis and asks Joe which wax would be best to use on them. Tyler expects a simple, straightforward answer to his question. Instead, he gets the history of wax and how it first came to be used on skis in the United States. Joe, with his preference for Intuition, likes global schemes and prefers novel and unusual suggestions, unaware of Tyler's preference for practical application. Can you see the potential for conflict?

Put yourself in the following role. You are an employee with a preference for Sensing. Your boss, an Intuitive type, has just told you that she wants you to develop a new product promotion package. She then launches into a long theoretical and abstract explanation of her vision of what the promotion should achieve.

Being a Sensing type, you want facts, details, and examples first and have many specific questions to ask. Suddenly, your boss stops in mid-thought and says to you, "I've got to run. I'm late for an important meeting." And out she goes, leaving you with the "sizzle" minus the "steak." It's a situation ripe for conflict or at least a load of frustration for you as the Sensing type.

Now, with the same Intuitive type boss, switch roles and play an employee with a preference for Intuition. As an Intuitive type, with a similar preference, a discussion of theory and abstractions with little consideration for practicalities at this point would probably resonate quite well. It would be a preference match with less potential for conflict.

Have you ever worked with someone who was so focused on the details of a project that you felt he lost sight of the goal? Or maybe you have worked with a person who asked so many questions she impeded the progress and slowed down the process. These Sensing type behaviors can annoy and frustrate Intuitive types.

So how can you avoid or at least minimize the potential conflict? You can use MBTI® preferences to create a climate where differences are seen as interesting and valuable rather than problematic. A shift in perspective can change your perception like the slight twist of a kaleidoscope. It depends on your attitude and approach.

> **Have you ever worked with someone who was so focused on the details of a project that you felt he lost sight of the goal?**

Look for the positive in the situation. As an Intuitive type, dismissing the details would create a problem because you can easily overlook information critical to your success. Appreciating the value of detail allows you to appreciate what Sensing types bring to the table. They read the fine print, are reliable, accurate, fill in the gaps, and, many times, cover for others.

As a Sensing type, dismissing theory and abstractions may be a rush to judgment and may put you in a situation of possibly not understanding the larger vision. Valuing Intuitive types' enthusiasm and big-picture view allows you to appreciate what they bring to the table. Those who prefer Intuition focus on the future, display creativity and imagination, and present unusual solutions that can be put to practical use.

Talk that matters promotes understanding by speaking the language of a different preference. You may even want to think of it as learning and practicing a foreign language.

•   •   •

Today try this experiment. If you have a preference for Intuition, find a friend or family member who has a preference for Sensing. Then, practice the language of details, specifics, and practicalities with him or her. Remember that this is how your friend or family member takes in information about the world.

If you have a preference for Sensing, find an Intuitive type and practice the language of theory and abstractions and vision with him or her because this is how your friend or family member perceives the world.

Pay special attention to the response you get. What do you notice? Is there more of a connection? How comfortable is your communication?

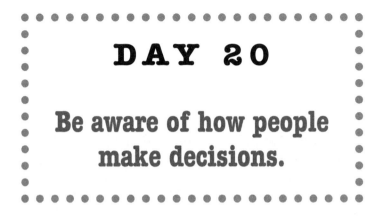

# DAY 20

## Be aware of how people make decisions.

Today we look at the Thinking-Feeling dichotomy of the MBTI® personality instrument. It describes how people make decisions. If someone asked you how you make a decision, could you explain your approach?

The Thinking-Feeling dichotomy offers two preferences for deciding. One is a preference for Thinking; the other is a preference for Feeling. Those who prefer Thinking make their decisions based on a clear, objective set of criteria. Those with a preference for Feeling use their values and instincts as criteria. Keep in mind that Feeling in this context does not mean emotion as much as it means instinct.

For example, when Jill, who has a Thinking preference, shops for a dress, she has certain criteria in mind for the dress she wants to buy. It must be a certain color, style, size, fabric, fit, and price. She walks into a store, finds a selection of dresses, and begins to evaluate each dress against her established criteria. If a dress meets all of the criteria, she buys it. If it doesn't, she leaves and goes to another store.

Becky, on the other hand, is a Feeling type and will use her values and instincts to make a decision. For Becky, the dress has to strike her fancy. If the dress feels good and makes her look sophisticated, it is a sale. Becky relies on a gut feeling, or instinct, for guidance.

The same process plays out if you're buying a car. If you are a Thinking type, before you even look at what is available, you first determine a set of criteria important to you. The list might include performance, gas mileage, sunroof, size, weight, handling, comfort, value, and safety, among others. Next, you go look at cars, kick some tires, do some road testing; and then you compare the cars to your criteria. Those that meet the criteria are contenders. Those that do not are eliminated.

If, on the other hand, you're a Feeling type, you decide based on your personal set of values and your instincts about the car. If the car makes you feel smart, prestigious, fashionable, "in," competitive, happy, powerful, or if you just like the color, look, and feel of the vehicle, then that is your basis for deciding.

How does the way you make a decision become a potential communication conflict and a hindrance to talk that matters? Let's say you and your spouse need to purchase a new computer for your home. As a Thinking type, you first compile a list of specifications you want in your computer. Next, you spend time on the Internet researching options and determining which models meet your specifications. You may even go to the store to test drive these products.

Your spouse, on the other hand, is a Feeling type. She's spotted the computer she wants to buy on the Internet and likes the look of it. She wants to buy the computer immediately and does not understand why you are dragging your feet. After all, the special sale lasts for two days only. Your spouse's values for aesthetics and saving money and her instinct for getting a "deal" are driving her decision making.

A potential conflict is brewing. So what can be done? If you are concerned with talk that matters, attempt to talk the language of the opposite preference. Talking from the other's perspective will help you better understand your mate's thought processes. For starters, simply acknowleging that each partner has a different preference for deciding can help. The next step is to surface the factors that are really important to each of you. And then, in a cooperative effort, put your heads together, and create a joint decision that incorporates what is truly important to both of you.

• • •

Today observe three important people in your life, and see if you can determine how they prefer to make their decisions.

> In a cooperative effort, put your heads together, and create a joint decision that incorporates what is truly important to both of you.

Do they have a preference for Thinking or Feeling? On what do they base their decisions? How do you connect with those of the same preference? How do you relate to those who are unlike you? List a few ways you might relate better to those whose decision-making preference differs from yours.

To get you started,[1] carry out the directions below:

1. Select words from the following list that describe a preference for Thinking. Mark them with a "T."
2. Then, select words descriptive of those who prefer Feeling and mark them with an "F."

Compare your answers to those at the bottom of the page.

| | | | | |
|---|---|---|---|---|
| objective | involved | social values | firm-minded | appreciative |
| laws | harmony | stability | humane | just |
| persuasion | clarity | circumstances | analytical | tenderhearted |
| policy | subjective | detached | critical | fair |

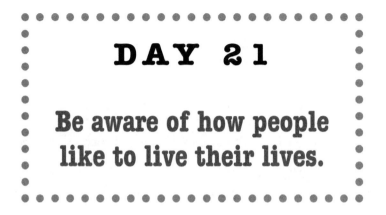

# DAY 21

## Be aware of how people like to live their lives.

The way we live our lives also impacts our attempts to engage in talk that matters. Do you prefer spontaneity in your life, or do you prefer to operate on a schedule? This chapter looks at the Judging-Perceiving dichotomy of the MBTI® personality assessment, which describes how people like to live their lives.

If you prefer flexibility and like to let life happen, believing everything will work out without having a detailed plan, you may be a Perceiving type. If you prefer to manage your time, have a schedule, and make lists of things to do, you probably have a preference for Judging.

Planning a vacation often demonstrates the difference in this particular pair of opposite preferences. For example, Paul and Rachel have been married for ten years and are planning a special anniversary trip to Las Vegas. Paul prefers flexibility in his life. Rachel has a preference for structure and schedules. How does this play out?

As a Perceiving type, Paul may feel that planning this holiday is a laborious task and may procrastinate about making plans. His tendency is to start at the last minute and let things happen as they may. Paul feels comfortable staying open to additional experiences, not wanting to miss anything. After all, isn't there something more exciting about driving and finding the "perfect" hotel on the strip on the spur of the moment?

This approach can be maddening for Rachel with her preference for organization and closure. She does not want to be caught at the last minute, having to scramble for a place to stay. She wants the arrangements made ahead of time, so she has the security of knowing what, when, where, and how their holiday will unfold. Rachel may feel secure with this level of structure, but Paul, with his preference for spontaneity, thinks the lack of flexibility may diminish the fun of their vacation.

How can Paul and Rachel use talk that matters to head off the conflict arising out of their different ways of living life? First, they can acknowledge and appreciate that the two of them have very different preferences about living. Second, they can ask questions of each other to determine: (a) the critical must-haves for Rachel, the Judging type; and (b) what will be fun for Paul, the Perceiving type. Third, collaboratively, they can develop a plan that meets both sets of needs. Talk does matter. How you practice it creates the results you want.

If you are a Judging type associated with a Perceiving type who wants to leave all the options open, recognize that he or she can change. Being better organized and more punctual is possible. Instead of shutting down communication or blaming this person, try inviting him or her to help plan ahead and create a loose schedule. Compromise will ease some of the tension between you.

If you happen to be a Perceiving type and associate with a person who prefers Judging, ask for patience. Explain that you feel boxed in when plans are settled on in advance and that you need room for spontaneity. You can acknowledge the advantages of planning and organizing but keep on the table your need for freedom to change plans.

Here is another example of how the Judging-Perceiving dichotomy can cause conflict. Betsy is an administrator in a public school. She is good at getting things done. Her boss once said, "She's the best administrator I have ever worked with." Yet volunteers have great difficulty working with Betsy. Because she is a Perceiving type, she simply does not plan ahead. Instead, she tells her volunteers, "We'll get it done. Everything will fall into place." Even when an activity has not been fully organized, she can pull things together and make it work. She gets the job done. But she also aggravates the life out of her volunteers. So deep is their frustration that Betsy now is having difficulty enlisting volunteers.

How would knowledge of the Judging-Perceiving dichotomy help Betsy and her volunteers? For one thing, they could discuss their different ways of functioning and then seek compromises. Perhaps the planning function could be delegated to a Judging type, someone who is adept at planning. Then Betsy can attend to all the spur-of-the-moment details that invariably arise.

•   •   •

Today look at those close to you at home and at work. Which of your family, friends, and coworkers are Judging types? How do you know? What behaviors give you clues?

Who are the Perceiving types? How can you tell? How do their preferences affect your relationship with them?

What conflicts arise in the relationships because of the difference in the way you like to live your lives? Ask each person what you can do to help ease the tension and enhance the relationship.

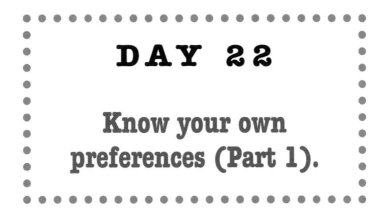

# DAY 22

## Know your own preferences (Part 1).

**T**o engage in talk that matters requires an awareness of how you relate to the world. Which of the following behaviors resonate with you?[1]

If you are an **Introverted** type, you probably

Rehearse things in your head before saying them and prefer that others do the same. For example, you often say, "I'll have to think about that" or "Let me get back to you on that."

If you are an **Extraverted** type, you probably

Tend to talk first, think later, and don't know what you will say until you hear yourself say it. For example, when collaborating on a project, you verbalize your thoughts and stop periodically to ask, "Does that make sense to you?"

If you are a **Sensing** type, you probably

Prefer specific answers to your specific questions. For example, when you ask someone what time it is, you prefer to hear "twelve fifty-five," rather than "a little before one" or "almost time to go."

If you are an **Intuitive** type, you probably

Look for possibilities, meanings, and the relationships between and among various things. For example, when taking a statistics class, you may have a difficult time accepting the formulas at face value and memorizing them. Instead, you may wonder, "Why do it that way? What significance does this formula have?"

If you are a **Thinking** type, you probably

Are impressed with and give more credence to things that are logical and scientific. Until you receive more information to justify the benefits of this book's concepts, you may be skeptical about their effectiveness.

If you are a **Feeling** type, you probably

Prefer harmony to clarity. For example, you may be embarrassed by conflict in groups or family gatherings. You may try to avoid conflict with phrases like "Let's change the subject," or try to smother it by saying, "Let's kiss and make up." If you find yourself in conflict with an in-law, you may let the issue slide by changing the subject and never addressing it again.

If you are a **Judging** type, you probably make statements like this:

"The movie was spectacular, although just a bit too long."

"I think the movie's photographers deserve some kind of a special award for the cinematography."

"Don't miss this one!"

As a **Judging** type, you have a tendency to evaluate—to make decisions and draw conclusions—rather than continue to take in new information.

If you are a **Perceiving** type, you probably make statements like this:

"I saw that movie you're raving about last week."
"That movie is getting a lot of press."
"I noticed it's only playing at a few select theaters."

In these statements, no judgments are made. They are simply statements with no implied evaluation. The Judging-Perceiving dichotomy is the easiest to detect and also seems to be the source of the greatest amount of interpersonal tension. Why? This preference most affects how we interact with others, and it is difficult to hide on a day-by-day basis.

•   •   •

Today think about which of these behaviors resonate with you. Can you trace any interpersonal tension at home or at work to conflicting preferences? If your answer is yes, spend fifteen minutes writing down ways you can help ease that tension, and then act on at least one of your ideas.

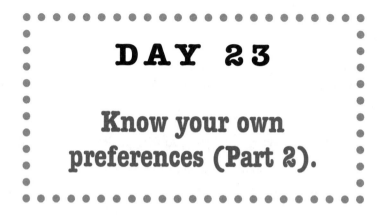

# DAY 23

## Know your own preferences (Part 2).

Review the words below in each pairing of preferences. Think about which column of words best describes you. Then, circle the preference at the top of that column. The words that resonate will give you an indication of your preferences. If it seems a toss-up, ask a friend or family member to help you. Have that person read the vignettes in the previous principles and the brief descriptions below to help you decide.

### What is your preference on the E–I scale?

| EXTRAVERSION (E) | INTROVERSION (I) |
| --- | --- |
| External | Internal |
| Outside thrust | Inside pull |
| Blurt it out | Keep it in |
| Breadth | Depth |

| | |
|---|---|
| Work more with people and things | Work more with ideas and thoughts |
| Interaction | Concentration |
| Action | Reflection |
| Do-think-do | Think-do-think[1] |

## What is your preference on the S–N scale?

| SENSING (S) | INTUITION (N) |
|---|---|
| The five senses | Sixth sense, hunches |
| What is real | What could be |
| Practical | Theoretical |
| Present orientation | Future possibilities |
| Facts | Insights |
| Using established skills | Learning new skills |
| Utility | Newness |
| Step by step | Leap around[2] |

## What is your preference on the T–F scale?

| THINKING (T) | FEELING (F) |
|---|---|
| Head | Heart |
| Logical system | Value system |
| Objective | Subjective |
| Justice | Mercy |
| Critique | Compliment |
| Principles | Harmony |
| Reason | Empathy |
| Firm but fair | Compassionate[3] |

## What is your preference on the J–P scale?

| JUDGING (J) | PERCEIVING (P) |
|---|---|
| Planned | Spontaneous |
| Regulate | Flow |
| Control | Adapt |
| Settled | Tentative |
| Run one's life | Let life happen |
| Set goals | Gather information |
| Decisive | Open |
| Organized | Flexible[4] |

When you have selected your preferences, enter them on the four lines below.

\_\_\_\_  \_\_\_\_  \_\_\_\_  \_\_\_\_

Now, compare your preferences above with the "best guess" you made on Day 17 (page 93). What do you discover?

•   •   •

We recommend you take the Myers-Briggs Type Indicator® (MBTI®) instrument published by CPP, Inc. because it is the only way to determine your true type. For more information on how you can take the assessment, go to www.mbticomplete.com, or contact:

CPP, Inc.
1055 Joaquin Rd., 2nd Floor
Mountain View, CA 94043
Toll Free: (800) 624-1765

# TIME OUT

## Review your progress.

Take time now to review the following behaviors that describe the pairs of opposites in each of the four dichotomies of the MBTI® personality inventory. If you familiarize yourself with the different behaviors, they will help you talk to and listen to others. We all have preferences. If you know what those preferences are, you can more effectively engage people in conversation, especially in talk that matters. As you reflect on the behaviors in each dichotomy, write down the name of a person you know who demonstrates those behaviors.

An **Extraverted** type is energized by the outside world of people, activities, and events. He or she will likely

- greet people easily;
- choose to work with others;
- talk over events and ideas with others readily;
- share his or her opinions readily;

- share personal experiences readily;
- have a relatively short attention span;
- attend eagerly to interruptions;
- act quickly, sometimes without thinking.

An **Introverted** type is stimulated by his or her own impressions, thoughts, and ideas. It is likely that he or she will

- choose to work alone or with one person;
- pause before answering;
- show discomfort with spontaneous questioning;
- spend time in thought;
- prefer quiet space for work;
- prefer jobs that can be done "inside the head";
- dislike interruptions;
- have a small number of carefully selected friends.

**Sensing** types use the senses of taste, touch, smell, hearing, and sight to understand the world. It is likely they

- are realistic and practical;
- are more observant than imaginative;
- prefer memorizing to finding reasons;
- learn best from an orderly sequence of details;
- are interested in facts and what is really true;
- keep accurate track of details;
- make lists;
- like to know the "right way" to solve problems.

Those who prefer **Intuition** take in the world around them by reading between the lines and imagining what might be. It is likely they

- enjoy new things;
- are more imaginative than observant;
- attend more to the whole concept than to details;
- are initiators, promoters, and inventors of ideas;
- see possibilities that others miss;
- dislike precise work with many details;
- don't always hear others out; anticipate others' words;
- are quick to find solutions.

**Thinking** types have a preference for organizing and structuring information and deciding in a logical, objective way. It is likely they

- want logical reasons before accepting new ideas;
- are impersonal, impartial, and try to be fair;
- are more truthful than tactful, if forced to choose;
- find ideas and things more interesting than people;
- are brief and businesslike;
- hurt others' feelings without knowing it;
- hold firmly to a policy or conviction;
- take seriously facts, theories, and the discovery of truth.

**Feeling** types decide in a personal, values-oriented way. It is likely that those with this preference

- are more interested in people than things or ideas;
- enjoy warm, personal relationships;
- are more tactful than truthful, if forced to choose;
- permit feelings to override logic;
- forecast how others will feel;

- arouse enthusiasm;
- value harmony and are upset by conflicts;
- relate well to most people.

Those who prefer **Judging** like to live life in an organized, planned, and structured way. It is likely they

- like to have things decided and settled;
- live according to plans;
- abide by a set of standards and customs;
- are uneasy with unplanned happenings;
- set up "shoulds" and "oughts" and judge themselves against them;
- are orderly, organized, and systematic;
- like assignments to be clear and definite;
- aim to be right.

Those who are **Perceiving** types like to live spontaneously with room for flexibility. It is likely they

- are more curious than decisive;
- live according to the moment;
- are comfortable handling the unplanned and unexpected;
- sample more experiences than can be digested or used;
- postpone unpleasant jobs;
- start too many projects and have difficulty finishing them;
- want to understand things more than manage them;
- adopt a live-and-let-live attitude.[1]

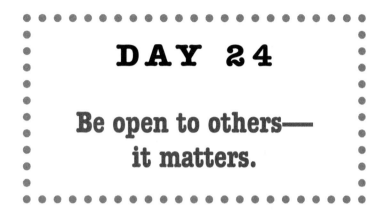

# DAY 24

## Be open to others— it matters.

**N**othing affects us more than how we see others—our images of them. These images determine what our emotions and attitudes toward others will be and, ultimately, how we will relate to them.

Kathy worked as a cashier in an airport shop. As a man came into her shop, she immediately noticed his tank top and shorts. He had a tattoo on his right arm from shoulder to elbow—a dagger with snakes surrounding it. On his left forearm was a tattoo of a large heart with an arrow piercing it. His bare feet seemed to confirm Kathy's image of this man. She quickly classified him as a hippie radical, teetering on the edge of society. He was the kind of person that she normally shunned.

The man picked up four AA batteries, a pack of tissues, and a newspaper and placed them on the counter. Instead of the angry rebelliousness she expected from him, he flashed a wide smile showing his pearly white teeth. He spoke in a soft, appealing voice as he asked about Kathy's day, and then he thanked her profusely. The man's warm, unassuming interaction with Kathy erased her negative image. She even wished him a good day.

When Kathy first saw this barefoot, tattooed man, she was prepared to have as little contact with him as possible. But his warmth, openness, and friendly smile quickly erased her original image of him. Unfortunately, most first impressions do not have such happy endings.

A cashier interacting with a customer represents the type of encounters that you experience many times a day. New people come into your life all the time. With some you have visual contact; with others you nod or gesture; and with others you can have meaningful conversations. In each instance, you form images and opinions of these people. And the image you hold affects your positioning, emotions, and attitudes—your interaction with them.

To build positive images for good relationships, use the PEA Approach: positioning, emotions, and attitude. Let's start with the P: **positioning**. Generally, when you meet people, you evaluate them and position them on a ladder in relation to yourself. For instance, if the person is a graduate of Yale, a bank president, an actor, or a wealthy philanthropist, you probably elevate this person and position him or her a rung or two higher on your ladder.

By contrast, if you meet a garbage collector, a cab driver, a convenience store clerk, or a store cashier, you might be tempted to position him or her on a lower rung on your ladder. None of us likes to think we evaluate people like this, but we do. A healthier response to a stranger would be to withhold judgment and initially position that person on the same rung of the ladder as you, as someone you would like to meet and get to know. Although a better first response, it often is not an easy one.

The E in the PEA Approach is **emotions**. How I see you can determine how I feel about you. The image you form of someone evokes an array of emotions within you. What emotions do you imagine Kathy experienced upon seeing the barefoot customer? And what about the customer's emotions as he approached her? You can experience a limitless range of emotions when meeting new people. Consider these:

- Openness
- Acceptance
- Fear
- Anxiety
- Caution
- Trust
- Curiosity
- Questioning
- Welcoming

Which of these emotions do you suppose Kathy felt as she saw the customer? Anxiety? Caution? Fear? What do you think the man felt as he approached Kathy? Openness? Curiosity? Trust?

The A in the PEA Approach is **attitude**. Attitude is stronger and longer lasting than positioning or emotions. By attitude we mean a basic orientation toward life. For example, one person may face life with fear and suspicion, but another sees the world as a safe, adventuresome place in which to live. One sees the glass as half empty and the other as half full. Both of these basic attitudes affect how you see others and your resulting relationships.

An attitude of openness toward others can help you see them in a positive light and experience the potential of relationship. Those who are open receive each day and each person who comes into their lives as gifts. They expect life to be good—and it often is. Of course, your attitude of openness will be tested, so here are a few affirmations to help you on those days. Read and repeat them to yourself often so you will be prepared for the inevitable bumps in the road.

- I will take persons who come into my life at face value. I will try to see them as they are and celebrate their uniqueness.
- I will postpone a hasty judgment. Before positioning them I will avoid evaluating them until I have heard them speak or act.
- I will find appropriate ways to relate to new people because each person and situation will call for different behaviors.
- I will ensure that my response truly is *my* response and not one conditioned by my parents' or society's values.

Think about your basic orientation to other people. How do you *see* them? Do you take them at face value? Do you postpone evaluation?

Or, if you carry negative images of others, how can you dissolve these images? There is no quick solution. You did not develop these negative attitudes overnight; beginning to see in a different light will take effort, practice, and persistence.

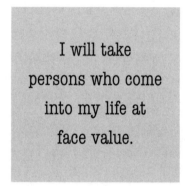

I will take persons who come into my life at face value.

Let's say you are given a new work assignment. Your boss places you with a person you do not know, and your first impression is negative. Here are some ideas to ease your negative feelings toward this colleague:

1. Ask yourself why you feel like you do. Have you experienced this feeling before? Is your response appropriate, or are you practicing an old habit?
2. Look for behaviors in this person that contradict your initial impression. In other words, look for the good instead of the bad.
3. Find new ways to relate to this person. Perhaps talking with him more often or listening to her problems will change your attitude.

4. Try acceptance. You may discover that your initial image was right. The person's behavior may be thoughtless, inconsiderate, and abrasive. Choose to accept him or her in the present condition, but do not let your negativity control you.

•   •   •

Today write down the names of the important people in your life. Note how you position them—same as you? above? below? Name your emotions toward them. Consider the emotions named on page 121, or use your own vocabulary to name your feelings.

Today also notice your image of every new person who comes into your life. Pay attention to how you position these people. Make notes to determine if you see an emerging pattern.

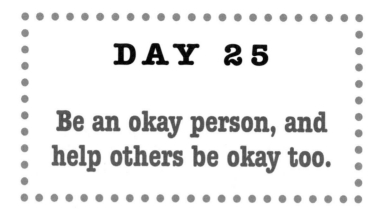

# DAY 25

## Be an okay person, and help others be okay too.

**B**en always carried himself in a way that created an easy atmosphere and nurtured the spirits of people he met. You have known folks like Ben—positive, outgoing, and contagious. Unlike Ben, many of us lack the feelings of okay-ness that make life full and rich. We tend to pick up every signal of acceptance or rejection. It is as though we are always asking, "Do you like me? What do you think of me? Am I safe with you?"

We do not feel good about ourselves and, because of this, we experience all the liabilities of low self-esteem. Most of us need positive verbal reinforcement for our sense of worth. But we also need to learn how to nurture good feelings about ourselves from within. We feel good when other people say good things about us, and we need to learn how to accept their gifts. Likewise we feel strengthened when we listen to our own inner affirmations.

If you want to sustain significant relationships, then engage in talk that matters. Look for the positive in others. State it. And repeat it. But be sincere, not manipulative.

Most people receive nurture when they are appreciated, listened to, and valued. When they hear positive, affirming words, they drop their guard and listen. But when they feel blamed, criticized, or judged, they feel threatened and will usually withdraw into a shell. People who live in shells do not communicate well.

Some years ago Thomas A. Harris wrote *I'm OK—You're OK*[1], in which he defined four positions people take in relationship to each other:

1. I'm Not OK—You're OK
2. I'm Not OK—You're Not OK
3. I'm OK—You're Not OK
4. I'm OK—You're OK

Not OK people lack positive self-images. Generally, early life experiences set the Not OKs on a road to self-rejection and anxiety. Over and over their life experiences confirm their negative view of themselves. Even when life affirms them, they read it as rejection.

If you supervise a Not-OK person, how do you offer him or her corrective suggestions without undermining confidence? How can you avoid confirming negative self-images? Suppose an employee reported to work late three days in a row. After examining his time card more closely, you discover that he is ten to twenty minutes late half the workdays a month. How can you tell him to be on time in a helpful, nonjudgmental way?

You do not want to approach it like this critical supervisor: "For weeks I've been noticing your late arrivals. Do you think you're a privileged employee who can come to work any time he pleases?" If you address the problem like this, you probably will not get the desired results. You will put the employee on the defensive and compromise job performance.

One approach is to be straightforward and say, "I see you've been ten to twenty minutes late more than half the days this past month. You know you need to be on time, and you know the importance of being on time to the team. What seems to be the problem?"

Or, if you know that the employee has a load of Not-OK feelings, you could begin with an affirmation. "You're a good worker; your production is strong, and the quality of your work is excellent. I appreciate your contribution to the company's success, which is why I'm concerned about your lateness this month. You know it's important to be at work on time. What's causing you to be late so often?"

> Criticism and blaming, even when softly labeled as constructive criticism, do not enhance the atmosphere for wholesome relationships.

The positive way is always the best. It lets you focus on the person and on the situation. Both are important if you hope to succeed in correcting behavior. Dealing with people in a negative way can create negative attitudes toward the job rather than creating change.

What have you accomplished if you forcefully correct the behavior but destroy morale, or if you affirm the person but do not correct the situation and fail to deal with the problem? Correcting or initiating change in behavior requires that you deal with the person *and* the situation. How many instances can you recall with an employee, a spouse, or a friend when you dealt with only one side of the issue—only the person *or* only the situation?

You may have used affirmation in a problem situation before but gotten nowhere. In fact, you can affirm some people until you run out of breath, and they simply do not hear you. But don't give up on affirmation; it is your best chance of succeeding.

Most of us must *learn* to be affirmative by appreciating our gifts and those of others. Unfortunately, the culture in which many of us were reared taught us to be defensive, critical, or silent. A competitive culture that honors winning at all costs leaves little room for the affirmation of others. Others become the enemy. How can "me first," "I'm the best," and "my way or the highway" give birth to talk that matters? These attitudes blind us to anyone's worth but our own. So what is left for others but a halfhearted recognition of their presence? Criticism and judgment of others follow closely on the heels of our own exalted sense of place. In this scenario, others serve as stepping-stones to our success.

Be assured that criticism and blaming, even when softly labeled as constructive criticism, do not enhance the atmosphere for wholesome relationships. Avoid this behavior if you want to communicate clearly. Here are four reasons why criticism and blame seldom work:

1. They create anxiety and emotional shutdown.
2. They confirm the other's negative self-image.
3. They focus on one side of the problem only.
4. They leave both parties helpless to move forward.

Louise knows how to affirm the people around her. Her affirmations have changed her relationships and brought her success. When she was in her fifties, she earned a job supervising a highly educated team with rather large egos. Many wondered if she had the maturity and experience to stand at the helm of such an important and complicated endeavor.

When Louise arrived on the job, her first act was to visit each of these high-powered, scholarly leaders. She asked personal questions. She listened. She responded to every positive revelation or achievement that she learned. She opened her life to them and invited direction and help.

In three months Louise had achieved the respect of her colleagues, along with an openness and clarity about the tasks to which they were committed. The environment changed from one of competition to cooperation. Trust in her leadership and her commitment to affirming every person's worth began to pervade the whole organization.

This woman did not bring to her task an intricate knowledge of each of the fields of learning represented by those she supervised. She did not assume that she could tell these highly respected academics how to do their work. But she did bring an ability to listen and a commitment to affirm those with whom she worked. Her example changed the style of communication and the atmosphere of that workplace.

Affirming others begins with recognition of your own deficiencies as well as your attributes. It is hard to affirm others if you cannot first affirm yourself. Look for the good in others. What do they do well? Which of their ideas have merit? What strength in them can you commend? Look for these attributes in others and clearly identify them.

State what you see. Say it, and then say it again. People often do not hear affirmation offered to them, so repeat it until they hear it. Even when they hear your affirmation, they may discount it with, "It was nothing; anyone could have done that."

When you need to correct someone or when you are seeking cooperation from a friend or a spouse, begin with an affirmation. After the affirmation ask for permission to make your suggestion. For example: "I like your urgency to get the sale completed. May I suggest what I believe will help? When you are unsure of the details or the time of delivery, give me a call. I will provide all the help I can." Once you have made the suggestion, then offer to help. An offer of help keeps the lines open and narrows the distance between you and the other person.

•   •   •

Here are three suggestions for learning to be an affirming person. Try them out today.

1. Think of yourself as an OK person. What helps you most to think that about yourself?

2. Look for a person in your life who needs words of affirmation.

3. Observe what happens when you begin to speak of the good you see in others.

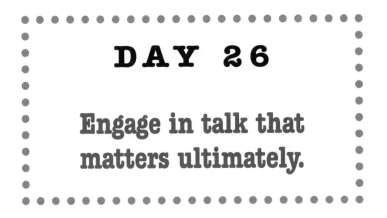

# DAY 26

## Engage in talk that matters ultimately.

One conversation matters more than all the others. Sometimes this conversation is nothing more than listening. At other times, it is thought without any boundaries. And at other times, this communication is filled with emotion and meaning. Let's look at talk that matters ultimately as it relates to other kinds of talk.

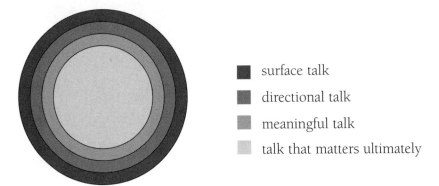

■ surface talk

■ directional talk

■ meaningful talk

□ talk that matters ultimately

The outermost circle represents **surface talk**. This is the chitchat that we engage in every day. When we say to others, "How are you?" we usually do not expect them to respond with a litany of their deep insights and feelings. You simply want them to reply, "I'm fine. How are you?" Talk like this has its place: it nurtures and holds together social relations. Even though fairly shallow, this type of communication keeps us in touch with others, lets us know that someone notices us, and makes us feel connected to one another.

Moving inward, the next circle represents **directional talk**. This has more substance than surface talk. Directional talk refers to the kind of talk a supervisor has with an employee or a parent has with a child. Directional talk makes suggestions, raises questions, asks for feedback, and attempts to affect the behavior of those addressed. Though an important form of talk, it is basically one-way talk.

**Meaningful talk,** the third circle, takes place when two people want to know and understand each other and are willing to take a few risks. Open dialogue like this often begins with surface chitchat and proceeds to sharing important ideas. Beyond the sharing of spontaneous remarks and studied thoughts, meaningful talk is a sharing of feelings—for example, failure, doubt, guilt, delight, and expectancy. This level of communication between two people is talk that matters.

In the innermost circle is **talk that matters ultimately**, which taps into a spiritual dimension. Spiritual talk turns our focus from human relations to God relations. You may not use the word *God*. Perhaps Creator, Absolute Being, Architect of the World, or Divine Mind may feel more comfortable to you. Or maybe you have made contact with the Ultimate through nature, beauty, aesthetics, or numbers and logic. Some speak of the transcendent as the Other or the Ground of Being. Talk that matters ultimately occurs in this dimension of human awareness.

You can be in contact with the Ultimate Power and Source of Life and Being in the universe. The manner of relationship with this Ultimate Being is called prayer, meditation, or contemplation. When you bring your daily life into conversation with this One whom many call God, amazing things can happen.

The most amazing aspect of being in contact with God lies in that relationship's ability to dispel loneliness. Perhaps for the first time, you realize that you are not alone, that someone is present with you in every moment of your life. This Transcendent One knows you, loves you, and desires the best for you.

This incredibly friendly Presence moves in your mind and imagination, furnishing images and ideas about your life, your future, and what gives you meaning. Indeed, this is a two-way relationship. You speak, and you are spoken to. Through the ages, humans have always believed that God speaks to them. God continues to speak to us today. If God speaks, we would do well to listen.

Conversation with God can include anything you want to talk about. Nothing in your life escapes God's interest and willingness to help. For instance, you can speak with God about blocked relationships and ask for help in clearing them up. You can share feelings of shame and guilt without fear of harsh judgment. You can unfold your hopes and dreams, knowing that God hears and understands your longings. You can face your fears and failures and find strength to continue your journey.

●　　●　　●

Even if this world of spirituality feels odd or new to you, here are some initiatives you can take to get started today in the ultimate conversation:

- Write a note to God as you would write to a close friend or family member. Write about your thoughts, feelings, and frustrations.
- If writing to God seems too strange or demanding, instead write about an event in your life. Reflect on one day of your life and describe where this Benevolent Power of Love had a hand in your

life. At first you may not perceive such an instance but keep reflecting on this aspect for a while.

- Ask the deeper questions in your life, such as: What is my life about? What is really important to me? How can I become who I am meant to be? Why do I keep longing for something more in life? These questions will likely press you up against the Love that sustains you.

- Try listening to the Voice within you. Speech is going on in the depth of your being. If you will only be silent and listen, you will hear it. Even dare to write down what you hear. Write as though Someone is speaking truth to you from deep within you. When you have written and read what you hear, respond to the Voice in writing. Make this a dialogue that goes on between you and the Ultimate Power and Meaning in life.

We recommend these efforts to enter into dialogue with God because we have tried them and found them fruitful. Begin to think of all your conversations as being in the presence of this Mystery and Power, and your talk will more fully be talk that matters.

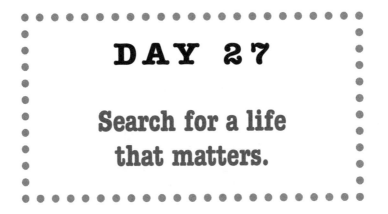

# DAY 27

## Search for a life that matters.

alk that matters comes from lives that matter. Seldom does meaningful talk issue from a chaotic life. The chaos demands too much attention, interrupts almost every conversation, and trivializes talk that otherwise might matter. There are discernible character traits in a life that matters, and these traits can be sorted out and embraced.

Perhaps the following parable will provide some insight. Long ago, a young man began to wonder, *What makes life matter?* He decided to ask those around him, those with experience. So first he asked his father. The father replied, "Respect and obey your father, a very ancient rule."

While the young man agreed with the sage advice, it did not seem like a complete explanation, so he sought out the chief elder of his clan. "What matters in life, and how can I lead a life that matters?" he asked.

The elder said, "Stay in the village, and never wander out to those settlements where the sun sets. And you should keep the laws and rules and observe the customs of the tribe. That will make your life matter."

The young man loved his tribe and appreciated its customs but felt there had to be something that made life richer, better, and more fulfilling than abiding by the ancient customs, laws, and rules.

The young man then visited the oldest and wisest person in the village. In answer to the question What makes life matter? the wise, old person paused, pondered, and finally spoke, "A life that matters honors the people that brought the life into the world—those with deep roots in the community and in society—but it goes far beyond that."

The ancient one was silent for a long time and then spoke. "I had the same questions when I was your age, and I was directed to an old hermit. This hermit has died, but there is another who lives in the mountain toward the setting sun. He can tell you."

Determined to find the answer, the young man set out to find the hermit in the mountain where the sun went down. He walked in the hot sun during the day and slept on the chilly ground at night. He trudged on for three days to the mountain.

As the path narrowed, the young man came upon a modest dwelling. In front of the small house sat the hermit, grinning and smoking a long-stem pipe.

"So," the hermit said, "you've come here searching for a life that matters?"

The young man was taken aback but nodded, hoping that he would be spared explaining himself. The old hermit with a vibrancy that contradicted his age and a clarity that left no room for doubt said, "I will tell you what makes a life that matters."

"First, accept and value yourself as a unique, unrepeatable miracle," he said. "There isn't anyone like you, and there never will be. To be you is something special.

"Second," he continued, "value the people in your life. Everyone is a child of the universe and has a place. While none is perfect, he or she is valuable nonetheless. Honor all feelings, and appreciate all thoughts and accomplishments.

"Third, discover your gifts, and use them in productive ways to create something of value for yourself and others," he said. "As you discover what you do best, what you love to do, and what others admire in you, you will find your direction to happiness and a life that matters.

"Fourth, always tell the truth. Nothing leads to chaos more quickly than misrepresentations, lies, and deception.

"Finally," the hermit concluded, "recognize that there is a power in you, a power greater than you that wants to energize your life, direct you, and lead you on the greatest adventure any human can experience. Some call this outside power Allah; others Yahweh; and still others, God. Whatever you call this power, find ways to be open to it and to be receptive to its work inside you, and you will be led into a life that matters."

> Discover your gifts, and use them in productive ways to create something of value for yourself and others.

When the hermit finished, he smiled and patiently observed the young man, for he knew that he now had a decision to make. The old hermit only wished that he could grant the young man a glimpse of the joy that awaited him and everyone who pursues a life that matters.

•   •   •

Today spend fifteen minutes alone thinking about the following question: How does this parable relate to my search for a life that matters?

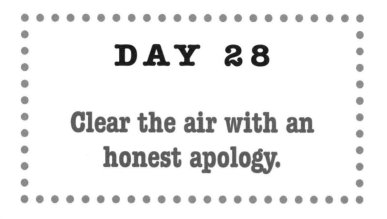

# DAY 28

## Clear the air with an honest apology.

If you are aiming for talk that matters, it will be important to keep the lines of communication open. All relationships accumulate tension, and yours are no different. If confusion, misunderstanding, and conflict continue, communication will become increasingly difficult.

You can take positive actions to relieve the tension. Recognize what is happening; verbalize it; take your share of responsibility; then offer a sincere apology. Let's look at each of these actions in more detail.

First, *recognize what is happening.* Jane, Amy, and Peter are all engaged in charitable work. Jane, forty-five, is the executive director; Amy, a volunteer in the organization, is retired; and Peter is a staff member. Peter asked Amy to work with him in creating a vision and a five-year strategic plan for the organization.

Over a couple of months, Amy noticed that Jane would withdraw from conversations with her. When Amy asked for a meeting, Jane was too busy. When Amy and Jane sat together in committee meetings, Jane did not acknowledge Amy's participation. After a few more weeks, Amy knew that the relationship was in jeopardy and had to be repaired or a deeper chasm would develop between the two of them. Amy took the first step and recognized something was happening.

Second, *verbalize your perceptions and ask for confirmation*. Finally, Amy knocked on Jane's door. Amy began the conversation by saying, "Jane, I've noticed some tension between us over the past few weeks, and I am unaware of why it has developed. Can you shed some light on this for me?" Amy took step two by verbalizing what she perceived and asking Jane for confirmation.

"Amy, I suppose that I need to make a confession to you. You have spent a great deal of time working with Peter developing a strategic plan for the next five years. I feel that strategy planning with staff is one of my responsibilities as executive director, and I have some negative feelings about you stepping into my role." Jane's candid reaction floored Amy, and for a few moments she remained silent, taking time to collect her thoughts.

When Amy finally gathered herself, she said, "I never thought about it like that, Jane. Peter invited my help. I gave it. It did not occur to me that you might have felt overlooked. Perhaps I did overstep my boundaries." With that statement of ownership, Amy moved on to step three: *take your share of responsibility*. She kept the door open for communication.

Fourth, *apologize*. Three magic words can clear the air: "I am sorry." Amy spoke these magic words to Jane; as a result, their work relationship continued without further misunderstanding.

Efforts to clear up a relationship can easily run aground. In Jane and Amy's situation, Amy could have kept silent with the hope that the tension would go away. Jane could have refused to acknowledge her own feelings, and the tension would have grown. When Amy offered her apology, Jane could have refused to accept it. Any of these actions would have added to the distance between the two women.

Offering an apology is just as important as recognizing and acknowledging. Apologizing means that you take a measure of responsibility, make yourself vulnerable, and show genuine concern for the other person. In a significant relationship, an apology is like an olive branch of peace.

Unfortunately, some apologies seem insincere, often driven by cultural expectation (this is what I was taught to say in a tense situation like this). Or, they are simply used out of habit. Still other apologies can be used to manipulate. Some sly communicators have learned that a quick apology sets up the other person to do their bidding. Using apology out of habit, for cultural reasons, or for manipulative purposes has no place in talk that matters. To clear the air, offer a sincere, heartfelt apology.

Consider the devastation that can occur when apologies are withheld, as the following story reveals. Don and Louise lived in the Midwest. Don, a successful businessman, had acquired a great deal of money and owned most of the stock in his growing company. He was generous to a fault with his two daughters, Mary Louise and Catherine. Mary Louise married well and did not need the money but accepted it anyway. Catherine did not marry as well, so the preinheritance helped her. Catherine also moved her family into a guesthouse on her parents' estate, although her father had reservations about the decision.

Three magic words can clear the air: "I am sorry."

As soon as Catherine and her family took up residence a few hundred yards from Don and Louise, Catherine began to issue orders to the caretaker. In addition, she told her parents' maid what miserable parents she had. Tensions developed. Catherine began to confront Don and Louise with greater frequency.

The climax came one Thanksgiving when Catherine groundlessly accused Don and Louise of being poor parents. She reviled both of them until they could endure it no longer. They asked her and her family to move out of the guesthouse. Reluctantly, they did. But Catherine continued her attack on Don and Louise by telling all their friends how she had been mistreated. Catherine also refused to let her children visit Don and Louise, telling the children that their grandparents were terrible people.

Despite efforts to deal with the tension, to put it on the table and resolve it, communication broke down completely. There were no face-to-face meetings, no telephone calls, no letters or e-mails.

Don concluded, "I suppose I've been too generous." Louise noted, "It is strange that Catherine has never been able to say 'I'm sorry' for anything." Instead of being hostile and ungrateful, Catherine could have eased the situation with an apology. But a sense of entitlement and a lifetime of self-will made an apology impossible for her.

Broken communication destroys relationships! Do you see what happens when the air is never cleared? Could a sincere apology have helped? We will never know, because Catherine never used the three magic words.

In contrast, apologizing and keeping communication open brings enormous rewards:

- You can work out differences.
- You can feel good about yourself and others.
- You can get rid of emotional garbage.
- You can live a happy, fulfilled life.

• • •

Today begin by thinking of one person to whom you owe an apology. Set a mutually convenient time when you can get together. Make an effort to resolve the conflict when you meet. State what you observe and ask for confirmation. Remember to use the three magic words: "I am sorry."

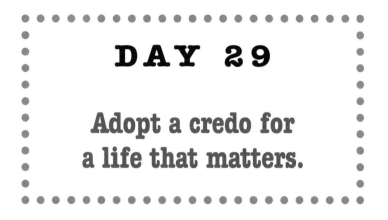

# DAY 29

## Adopt a credo for a life that matters.

To achieve a life that matters, you will need to adopt a credo or set of guiding principles. The following twelve statements will provide a springboard for thinking about the commitments you might wish to make. These twelve statements form a credo of belief and conviction. If you embrace them, or others like them, and practice them faithfully, they can supply more than talk that matters; they can offer you a *life* that matters.

1. I am committed to those actions that enable talk that matters.
2. I will send clear messages that express my ideas, my thoughts, and my feelings.
3. I will listen first.
4. I will attend to my feelings when engaged with another person so my unconscious reactions do not corrupt the relationship.
5. I will honor with respect and appreciation my partners in talk that matters.

6. I will ask for clarification or offer feedback to make certain that I understand what the other is saying.

7. I will try to negotiate disagreements and work for equitable resolutions.

8. I will engage people with openness and enthusiasm.

9. I will try to avoid conversations that criticize, blame, judge, or discount others.

10. I will have integrity in my talk, and I will refuse to manipulate or control others.

11. I will remember that relationships are my most treasured assets.

12. I will try to be aware that all conversation occurs in a sacred environment with meaning both for God and for me.

•   •   •

Today write the first draft of your personal credo. Put it aside for a week, and then review and revise it as needed.

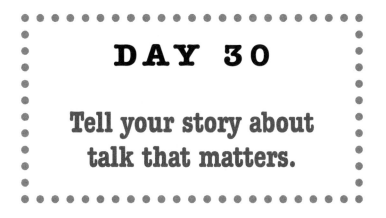

# DAY 30

## Tell your story about talk that matters.

T elling our stories about how we came to experience talk that matters will help others find their way into more rewarding relationships. Consequently, we (Susan and Ben) want to share our stories with you.

### Susan's story

My parents have been my inspiration for writing *Talk That Matters* and my role models for thoughtful and effective living. Early on, they taught me the importance of separating a person from his or her behavior, a concept that directly affected my self-esteem.

I recall when I was a child goofing around with my sister on the front steps of our home in Chicago. My parents warned us to stop, but we continued until I fell and broke my ankle. Rather than telling me I was clumsy or stupid, Mom and Dad said that stupid actions get stupid results, but they loved me nonetheless. They knew the resulting pain and inconvenience I experienced was enough punishment.

Mom and Dad presented a united front in their child rearing. What one said, the other supported. When one said no, the other agreed with the decision. I cannot recall a time when I was able to divide them and conquer. Their communication with each other was, and is, strong.

In high school, I fretted about whether I was popular with boys. When I started dating, I took my concern to my parents and asked them what I might talk about on a date to keep the conversation flowing and the boy interested. They wisely recommended that I ask questions to get the young man talking about himself—his interests, his family, his job, his friends, his hobbies. I followed their advice, and it held me in good stead. To this day, I use questions as a communication default. When I do not know what to say or do in a situation, I ask a question. It is amazing how it smooths the way and adds a ton of helpful information.

My parents told me that if I was going to ask questions of others, I needed to do something equally important—listen. I saw them model effective listening every night at the dinner table. When the five of us sat down together, each one of us had an opportunity to talk about his or her day without interruption. It was our time to shine, and my parents listened to what we said. It had a profound effect on me. I grew up feeling cared for, respected, and valued. Plus, I learned to listen effectively.

Another influence on the way I communicate is my belief that no one can hurt our feelings but us. During a period of struggle in my marriage, I realized that I can control how I feel. I can allow myself to feel okay about a situation; or I can choose to be sad, angry, or disappointed. Granted, someone can create an unpleasant environment for me, but I decide how I am going to respond to the person and the situation.

My dad's response to me during tough times growing up also greatly influenced the way I communicate. Those tough times included the pain of not making valedictorian, lying to a teacher and getting caught, and revealing too much personal information and humiliating myself. "Not to worry," Dad would say. "Let's sit down and talk about it." He had a way of letting me talk until my energy was expended and then adeptly guiding me into a plan of action.

I found a quote recently that accurately sums up my dad's approach as he coached me through those painful times: "In affairs of the heart . . . one should offer neither advice nor solutions . . . just a clean hanky when it seems appropriate."[1]

Together, Mom and Dad have been my communication role models. But more than this, they have instilled tremendous life values as well. They have taught me to

> Watch your thoughts; they become words.
> Watch your words; they become actions.
> Watch your actions; they become habits.
> Watch your habits; they become character.
> Watch your character; it becomes your destiny.
> —Author Unknown

## Ben's story

Susan and I have had different but complementary journeys into talk that matters. Growing up, I had a number of influences and experiences that contaminated the way I communicated. I struggled with low self-esteem and the fear that I was a nobody. In my adolescent years, I coped by hiding behind a persona that did not reflect who I really was. I found ways to function and to feel included in my group, but I never was comfortable with myself. My problems with openness and intimacy were compounded by a marriage that merged two very different people, both of whom lacked good communication skills. The marriage ultimately failed. Yet through the process of counseling and trying to save the marriage, I finally learned how to engage in talk that matters.

My journey into meaningful communication came one step at a time over a period of eight or ten years. Reading Thomas Harris's *I'm OK—You're OK* helped me see that I often found myself in painful relationships where I felt that "you're okay, but I'm not okay." Practicing Harris's suggestions began to have results in my life. I had found a path that led to acceptance of the person that I was.

Virginia Satir, author of *Peoplemaking*,[2] was another influence on my journey. Through her book, I came to see that blaming, placating, computing, and withdrawal all blocked meaningful talk.

At a workshop led by Satir, she told us, "You have a choice—you may continue to struggle as you are now, or you can learn ways that will work better for you." I applied that statement to myself, and I chose to change. She also said, "It has taken a number of years for you to become the person you are, and you will not likely change overnight." I learned that it was okay for me to be on a slow path and that relapses would probably occur (and they did), but I could persist until I learned how to engage in talk that matters.

Along the way I also met John Powell, one of the most authentic human beings I have ever known. I hungered for the same honesty and integrity I saw in him. In chapter 1 of his book *Why Am I Afraid to Tell You Who I Am?*, Powell related a moving story. One man said to him: "I am afraid to tell you who I am, because, if I tell you who I am, you may not like who I am, and it's all that I have."[3] That man confessed my fear. Often my telling this story to others in talks or workshops would move me to tears. I was afraid to be real because my real self might be rejected.

The person to whom I owe the most, perhaps even my life, is W. Burney Overton. Burney is no longer with us on this earth, but his influence and vision lives through hundreds of us whose lives he touched. Burney was a large, bald-headed, compassionate man. When my first marriage was in desperate trouble, he was recommended to us as a counselor. I liked Burney from the first day. He was real, open, caring, and without any judgment or condemnation. In our sessions, he focused on relational communication by helping two people hear each other and honestly express their feelings.

As the sessions went on, I discovered how sick the relationship was, and I decided to end the marriage for our sanity. But I continued to meet with Burney to find my way through to healing and wholeness. From him I learned most of the practices that I have written about in this book. In conferences, workshops, and retreats, I kept absorbing the principles of talk that matters, and they changed my life. Perhaps I might say they *saved* my life.

●   ●   ●

These are our stories. What is your story? Today, write about your journey so far toward talk that matters.

# Determine Your Progress

Score yourself on what you have learned in these thirty days. Below are fifteen questions. Read each one; reflect on your practice, then give yourself a grade. A 1 means you really missed the mark, and a 10 signifies you nailed it! When you have answered all the questions, total your score. You'll find an interpretation following the questions.

## Questions to Help You Evaluate Your Learning

1. How well have you learned to talk straight about your thoughts, feelings, and desires without hiding your true meaning? If you find yourself saying "some people" or "someone ought to" or if you report from sources outside the conversation, you likely are not

sending a straight message. If you score yourself below 7, again read Day 1, "Discover Where You Are."

**My Score:** 1   2   3   4   5   6   7   8   9   10

2.  How well are your instructions, e-mails, and written memos understood? Have you learned to write and speak clearly? If you need help with this concept, review the steps in Day 5, "Write a Clear Message."

**My Score:** 1   2   3   4   5   6   7   8   9   10

3.  How firmly do you stand in your own space, claim your own personhood, and speak your ideas forthrightly and clearly? If you discover that you frequently get queasy in a conversation, blame yourself for failures, and feel inferior in a relationship, review Day 10, "Talk Straight."

**My Score:** 1   2   3   4   5   6   7   8   9   10

4.  How well do you claim your power in a relationship? People who are insecure in a relationship often ascribe to the other person powers that he or she does not possess. If you discover that you are feeling uncertain about yourself, seeing others as all powerful or at least more powerful that you, review the different approaches in Day 11, "Stand Firm."

**My Score:** 1   2   3   4   5   6   7   8   9   10

5.  How well do you work at relationships to keep them healthy and growing? If you find that valued relationships frequently become testy, if you notice that friends and associates draw back from you, and if you find yourself willing to walk away from an important

relationship, seek an answer in Day 12, "Help Others (and Yourself) Speak Up."

My Score:   1   2   3   4   5   6   7   8   9   10

6.  How would you rate yourself on speaking positively in a delicate situation? All of us have occasions when we do not know the appropriate words to speak. If you seek to avoid hard situations and feel speechless when tragedy strikes, find help in Day 14, "Practice Supportive Speech."

My Score:   1   2   3   4   5   6   7   8   9   10

7.  How open are you to enlisting the help of a trusted friend to keep you accountable for your decisions to become a better communicator? If you find yourself making decisions to change and not following through, review Day 15, "Be Accountable for Your Speech."

My Score:   1   2   3   4   5   6   7   8   9   10

8.  How would you rate yourself in the use of authority? If you do not believe you have personal influence or if you have been promoted to a new position of authority over others, review Day 16, "Use Power and Position Wisely."

My Score:   1   2   3   4   5   6   7   8   9   10

9.  What are the various preferences in the Myers-Briggs Type Indicator? Give yourself 1 point for each preference you correctly name and 2 additional points if you can name all eight of them. If you

cannot name all of them, see Day 17, "Understand That People Are Different."

My Score:  1   2   3   4   5   6   7   8   9   10

10. What are the characteristics of an *extrovert*? of an *introvert*? Give yourself a point for each correct characteristic. Reread Day 18, "Be Aware of How People Are Energized," to check your answers.

My Score:  1   2   3   4   5   6   7   8   9   10

11. How do *sensing* and *intuition* differ? Give yourself 2 points for each difference you can cite. See Day 19, "Be Aware of How People Take in Information," for a refresher.

My Score:  1   2   3   4   5   6   7   8   9   10

12. How do *thinking* and *feeling* differ? Give yourself 2 points for each difference you can cite. See Day 20, "Be Aware of How People Make Decisions," for a review.

My Score:  1   2   3   4   5   6   7   8   9   10

13. How does *judging* differ from *perceiving*? Give yourself 2 points for every difference you can identify. See Day 21, "Be Aware of How People Like to Live Their Lives," if you need some help.

My Score:  1   2   3   4   5   6   7   8   9   10

14. What are two benefits of affirming communication? Give yourself 5 points for each answer. Day 25, "Be an Okay Person, and Help Others Be Okay Too," will stimulate your imagination.

My Score: 1    2    3    4    5    6    7    8    9    10

15. If you have written your credo for a life that matters (see Day 29) give yourself 10 points. If not, you score no points.

My Score: 0                                                    10

Add up your score.  Total: _____

## Your Score

In this final evaluation of your ability to engage in talk that matters, there are 150 possible points. If you scored 150 points, check that you are being totally honest with yourself. If you scored 135 points, consider yourself well on your way to being competent in meaningful talk. A score above 120 indicates that you have made significant progress, but you need to be more aware of what is occurring between you and other people. If you scored below 100, we encourage you to go back through the thirty days, rereading them carefully and practicing them more diligently, especially working hard on the daily exercises.

# Notes

### Before You Begin

1. Dan Hurley, "Divorce Rate: It's Not as High as You Think," *The New York Times* (April 19, 2005).

### Day 4

1. See Albert Mehrabian, *Silent Messages: Implicit Communication of Emotions and Attitudes,* 2nd ed. (Belmont, CA: Wadsworth, 1981).

### Day 7

1. Ernest Holmes, *The Science of Mind* (Sacramento, CA: Murine Pess 2006), 176.

### Day 8

1. *People Skills Learnt Right, Not Rote*SM, Interact Performance Systems, Inc. www.InteractPerformance.com / (800) 944-7553.

### Day 17

1. Sandra Krebs Hirsh and Jean M. Kummerow, *Introduction to Type in Organizations: Individual Interpretative Guide*, 3rd ed. (Palo Alto, CA: Consulting Psychologists Press, 1998), 1.

2. Mary H. McCaulley, et al., "The Myers-Briggs Type Indicator and Leadership" (prepared as a chapter in *Measures of Leadership: The Proceedings of a Conference on Psychological Measures and Leadership*, sponsored by The Center for Creative Leadership, and The Psychological Corporation, San Antonio, TX, October 23–26, 1988), 30–31.

3. See Isabel Briggs Myers with Peter B. Myers, *Gifts Differing: Understanding Personality Type* (Mountain View, CA: Davies-Black Publishing, 1995), 66, 182.

4. Ibid., 29.

**Day 20**

1. Based on information in Otto Kroeger and Janet M. Thuesen, *Type Talk: The 16 Personality Types That Determine How We Live, Love, and Work* (New York: Delta/Dell Publishing, 1989), 28.

**Day 22**

1. Adapted from Kroeger and Thuesen, *Type Talk*, 14–21, 39.

**Day 23**

1. Sandra Hirsh and Jean Kummerow, *LIFETypes* (New York: Warner Books, 1989), 21.

2. Ibid., 36.

3. Ibid., 50.

4. Ibid., 65.

**Time Out**

1. Gordon Lawrence, *People Types and Tiger Stripes: A Practical Guide to Learning Styles*, 2nd ed. (Gainesville, FL: Center for Applications of Psychological Type, 1982), 70–77.

**Day 25**

1. Thomas A. Harris, *I'm OK—You're OK: A Practical Guide to Transactional Analysis* (New York: Harper & Row, Publishers, 1969), 43.

**Day 30**

1. Arturo Pérez-Reverte, *The Flanders Panel*, trans. Margaret Jull Costa (New York: Bantam Books, 1996), 14.

2. Virginia M. Satir, *Peoplemaking* (Palo Alto, CA: Science & Behavior Books, 1972).

3. John Powell, *Why Am I Afraid to Tell You Who I Am?: Insights on Self-Awareness, Personal Growth and Interpersonal Communication* (Niles, IL: Argus Communications, 1969), 12.

# For Further Study

Adler, Ronald B. Lawrence B. Rosenfeld, and Russell F. Proctor. *Interplay: The Process of Interpersonal Communication*. 11th ed. New York: Oxford University Press, 2009.

Devito, Joseph A., *The Interpersonal Communication Book*. 12th ed. Boston, MA: Allyn and Bacon, 2008.

Robinson, Jonathan. *Communication Miracles for Couples: Easy and Effective Tools to Create More Love and Less Conflict*. Newburyport, MA: Red Wheel/Weiser, 2009.

Stewart, John. *Bridges Not Walls: A Book about Interpersonal Communication*. 10th ed. Burr Ridge, IL: McGraw-Hill Higher Education, 2008.

Trenholm, Sarah, and Arthur Jensen. *Interpersonal Communication*. 6th ed. New York: Oxford University Press, 2007.

Wilmot, William W., and Joyce L. Hocker. *Interpersonal Conflict*. 7th ed. New York: McGraw-Hill Companies, 2005.

# About the Authors

DR. BEN CAMPBELL JOHNSON is Professor Emeritus from Columbia Theological Seminary. He has earned his place by teaching communication and human relations for a number of years. He also has woven his insights into the church's outreach and growth in spirituality through stronger relationships. He has published over forty books on a variety of subjects. All the insights shared in this volume aim to help people understand and improve their ability to communicate with family, friends, and coworkers.

●　　●　　●

DR. SUSAN LEE LIND has more than twenty-five years of experience in the fields of interpersonal communication, training, and organizational development. She has delivered hundreds of workshops to a variety of businesses, nonprofit organizations, and governmental entities. Using assessment tools like the Myers-Briggs Type Indicator (MBTI®), the Reuven Bar-On EQi, and Situational Leadership, Dr. Lind has designed, developed, and delivered executive, managerial, and supervisory training; facilitated client work teams; and coached executives and managers, providing 360-degree feedback and individual development planning. *Talk That Matters* is a labor of love offered in the hope that those committed to enhancing their relationships will find the help they need within its pages.